Father
Your Son

Father
Your Son

*How to Become the Father
You Always Wanted to Be*

Stephan B. Poulter, Ph.D.

McGraw-Hill

New York   Chicago   San Francisco   Lisbon   London   Madrid   Mexico City
Milan   New Delhi   San Juan   Seoul   Singapore   Sydney   Toronto

I dedicate this book to all the men involved in the process of becoming the fathers they have always wanted. These fathers are increasing in number and influence every day. I also know this book would not have been written without the presence of four people in my life. No single event has shaped my life more dramatically than the birth and growth of my two lovely children, and for that I am very fortunate. Second, my parents are deeply in my heart for life. They have always given me the unspoken permission to make a difference in the world.

To Madison—my adorable daughter who first introduced me to fatherhood and its limitless potential and opportunity. Who has shown me the power of love, courage, and the secrets of being a woman. Who has the giftedness of a queen, the love of a nurturer, and the inner beauty of a young rose.

To Jonathan Brett—my precious son, who has the spirit of a warrior, the courage of a leader, the heart of a compassionate soul, and the wisdom of an old master.

To my parents—you gave me the chance to excel, and to pursue my dreams and desires regardless of the risk.

Contents

Acknowledgments

Though I don't have the space to acknowledge everyone who has helped me as a father, therapist, and author, I would like to single out some key individuals. These men and women have helped me to resolve my own fatherlessness and create this book.

The boys I grew up with: Brad Jenkins, Chris "Red" Casey, and Keith Costello are great influences in this book. My earliest mentors, Dave Lehr and Mike Jones, showed me hope and love. Mrs. Diane Jensen and Mr. Joe Casey, who told me when I was a high school senior to make something of my life. Dr. Jay Burger, who changed the course of my life by allowing me to attend the University of Southern California on a scholarship. Bob Barnes, Russ Hunter, Jack Hayford, Dennis Corrigan, Ed Goorjian, John Wimber, Robert Bly, and Neale Donald Walsh have contributed to my mentoring process and the creation of this book.

I am thankful for the law-enforcement days, seminary, and graduate school of my twenties, when survival wasn't a metaphor but a reality. Police officers, professors, and fellow psychologists who had seen another side of life were willing to share their wisdom about it with me. Some of these men included Brook McMahon, David Thompson, Duane Williams, Jim Mooney, Randy Sugg, Marvin Coven, and Gregg Britton.

I would also like to acknowledge my faithful agent, Jane Dystel, my tireless editor at McGraw-Hill, Barbara Gilson, Dr. Jane Semel, M.D., Laura Golden-Bellotti, Jon and Eileen Gallo, Betty Deones, Julia Wolfe, Denise Dugay, Dr. Winston Gooden, Rory Zaks, Bill Klem, Kye Hellmers, Ed McPherson, the late Marvin Zaks, William Perez, Barbara Zax, Marlene Clark, Bob Brody, and Carson and Bill Palmer.

I am also grateful to Bruce Wexler, who was able to focus, shape, and direct my writing and offered invaluable suggestions. Finally, I want to mention the thousands of fathers and sons who I have had the pleasure of speaking to about the most important man in their life: **Father.**

Introduction

While there are many bad fathers out there, you are probably not one of them. Bad fathers wouldn't be interested in a book like this. For all intents and purposes, they have given up, convinced that they are never going to measure up as fathers. Or they may just not care about being a parent. In my practice I have worked with and heard about deadbeat dads, physically abusive dads, and alcoholic and drug-addicted dads. These men have fled the responsibilities of being a father, and the effect on their children is devastating—but it is especially harmful to their sons. As I will emphasize throughout this book, dads have a critical role to play in the emotional, psychological, and spiritual development of their boys, a role that no mother—no matter how committed and caring she might be—can fulfill.

You do, however, have something in common with the bad dads. You, like they, are a son. You, like they, had a father who made mistakes. Perhaps your father wasn't as bad as theirs. Maybe he didn't beat or sexually abuse you. Maybe he didn't desert the family. Maybe in some respects he was a good father. But he made mistakes as a parent that affect how you raise your son. Whether he was verbally abusive, frequently absent, or emotionally uninvolved, he created a wound that has not healed. Although you may not be aware of it, this wound causes you to act toward your son in counterproductive ways.

Another problem is that you have never been taught how to be a father. The odds are that your own father didn't provide the perfect model and, in fact, may have perpetuated certain myths about fatherhood. One of the most common misconceptions involves the macho attitude toward raising boys. Many fathers refrain from displaying much emotion—with the possible exception of anger—toward their sons. They adopt an emotionally cold pose on the theory that they do not want to coddle their sons and thus leave them unprepared for the real world. The problem, of course, is that they fail to establish an emotional bond with their boys, harming both the relationship and their sons' ability to express their own emotions.

In your quest to be a good father, you face the handicaps of your heritage and your lack of knowledge. What will help you to overcome these handicaps is your desire to be a better father to your son than your father was to you. This impulse is why you are not content just to *be* a father. You are willing to reflect on your actions and recognize when you have done something wrong. You are interested in learning about how you can facilitate your son's passage through each developmental stage. And you are sufficiently motivated to be a good father that you have picked up a book that will help you to achieve that goal.

The Process: What You'll Learn and How to Use It

This book is essentially divided into two sections. The first section—Chapters 1 through 5—is all about preparation. At first you may wonder why you need to prepare. The male impulse is to take action, and you probably want to know exactly what you need to do to be a better father to your son. Unfortunately, I can't just tell you how to be a good father, and then you can implement it lickety-split. Your best intentions will be undermined by forces operating below the conscious level. You may want to spend more time going with your young son to playgrounds or you may want to avoid having daily screaming matches with your teenage son, but despite your resolve, you probably will fall back into these relationship patterns. This is so because you have unaddressed issues from your childhood that you need to confront. Don't worry. You don't have to undergo years of psychoanalysis to deal with these issues. You do, however, need to prepare for them by being more aware of what they entail and doing the types of exercises that will lessen their impact on your behaviors.

The first chapter is designed to help you assess how these buried issues may be affecting your parenting. You will find a number of exercises that will assist you in getting a handle on how your words and deeds are affecting your son, both positively and negatively. The next four chapters all focus on the fathering legacy that has been handed down to you not only from your father but also from your grandfather. The key is to identify how their parenting may have caused you emotional trauma and link this trauma to how you are as a father. As a result of your upbringing, you have adopted a certain style as a father, and in Chapter 4 we will explore how you can identify this style and be aware of its potential impact on your son. Chapter 5 will help you to let go of the "lost boy" inside who is pushing you toward a negative fathering style. All the chapters in this first section will make you a much more conscious father who is better equipped to manage the negative impact of your past.

The next group of chapters—6 through 10—focus on what you can do during each stage of your son's development, from the time your wife is pregnant through the end of adolescence. It doesn't matter what age your son is now. It is important for you to be aware of the mistakes you may have made when he was younger so that you can compensate for them at this point. It really helps to link your teenage son's actions to your parenting style when he was little; it gives you a sense of perspective on why he is the way he is and stops you from blaming him. It also provides you with insight about what you didn't give him then as a father and what you should be giving him now. As you will discover, each development period brings with it a unique set of challenges, and I have provided a great deal of information and a number of tools for you to meet these challenges. Three of these five chapters concentrate on adolescence because this is such a complex, difficult period for many fathers and sons, and there are specific things that you need to do and think about throughout your son's teenage years.

The book's final chapter provides a provocative perspective on the challenges to good fathering in a highly volatile and complicated world and how dads need to work with the mothers of their sons to raise boys with good values and a strong sense of their identities.

Each chapter will be filled with tools/tips and stories. The former will include everything from self-assessment quizzes to checklists to role-playing scenarios. They are designed to facilitate applying the book's information to your own life. I have tried as much as possible to avoid the psychological jargon that is fine for other therapists but off-putting to readers looking for insight and advice. Although I will introduce you to important psychological concepts, I have included numerous tools and techniques so that you can make practical use of these concepts.

You are also going to find many stories. Most have been taken from my practice, although I have also included stories that friends have told me, as well as my own experiences as a father. I have disguised the identities of the people in these stories, creating composite anecdotes at times. Still, you will recognize the all-too-familiar situations fathers and sons find themselves in and the difficult decisions dads must make. To this end, I would like to share two quick stories with you to illustrate the parenting issues dads face and how each one brings a different perspective and history to these issues.

Two Fathers Struggling with the Past and Present
Mike

Mike, 29, is a married professional with one child, 18-month-old Evan. Mike was a very devoted and involved father during Evan's first six months, spending a lot of floor time with his son. Mike's wife, Cheryl, though, has complained to him on a number of occasions that recently he has been spending a lot of time at work or playing golf with his friends on weekends instead of being with his son. Mike was only vaguely aware that he was drifting away from his son, and at first he told Cheryl that as the mother she had the lion's share of child raising. He felt that as a stay-at-home mom, she didn't appreciate how much pressure he was under to support the family and that he needed to get out and have fun every so often on weekends. By the time Evan was 18 months old, however, Mike realized that he was neglecting his son. As much as he loved Evan, he found himself worrying that he was a bad father, that there was something wrong with him because he was gone so much of the time. Deep down inside Mike realized that he had simply been offering his wife excuses about why he couldn't be around the house more. Something was driving him away, and it was only gradually that it dawned on him that his relationship with his own father had something to do with it.

Mike's dad, Richard, was a highly successful man, an entrepreneur who had built a chain of retail stores from scratch. Growing up, Richard had always made an effort to do things with Mike, especially sports. Richard had pushed Mike hard, insisting that he take private golf and tennis lessons. He also was on Mike all the time about his grades, chastising him whenever he received anything less than an A. There were times when Mike was growing up that he dreaded the sight of his father arriving home from work, knowing that he would be on his case seconds after he walked through the door.

Now, when he saw Evan, Mike realized that his avoidance of his son may have had something to do with his wish to avoid his father. Watching his son playing with blocks on the floor one day, he forced himself to get down on the floor and help him. It was difficult and uncomfortable, and he hated that feeling. Then, when Mike accidentally knocked down a tower that his son had built, Evan screamed for his mother, and Mike felt like an utter failure as a dad.

Sam

Sam, 42, is the father of 15-year-old Joshua, and he finds it difficult to deal with his son without getting into an argument. To Sam, it seems as if Josh stays up nights thinking of new ways to irritate him. In the past month Josh has been caught smoking on school grounds, told his father that he intends to drop out of high school at age 16 and get a job where he can make money, and started dating a girl who strikes Sam as incredibly immature and obnoxious. Although he tries to talk with Josh about these issues logically and dispassionately, their conversations always devolve into raised voices and accusations.

After these arguments, Sam feels tremendous remorse. He remembers what a great kid Josh was when he was little and how his son looked up to him. Sam would take him on outings to playgrounds, and they would have a great time. Back then he couldn't imagine he and Josh being anything but close. He would brag about his son to his friends at work and tell them what a smart, sensitive kid he had. Now, after an argument, Sam can't believe that he is remembering the same person. Teenaged Josh and 8-year-old Josh seem like two completely different people, and he beats himself up for having somehow "created a monster."

Eventually, Sam realizes that much of what Josh is going through is not just part of being a teenager but a necessary part. He learns that despite appearances, Josh feels close enough to his father to risk rejecting everything he stands for. Underneath his rebellious pose, Josh feels a strong enough attachment to his father that he knows that Sam will always love and support him. Sam also comes to understand that his own father, a passive type, had grown very distant during Sam's teenage years. He and Sam never argued, but they also never talked much, and Sam begins to see that his father never modeled father-son communication for him. To a certain extent, this lack of a model makes him struggle when trying to talk to his volatile, rebellious teenager. And when he struggles, he gets mad at himself and usually turns this anger loose on Josh.

The good news is that both Sam and Mike figured out how to be better fathers to their sons. They became more aware of how to handle their boys at the different stages of development—they learned what to expect and the positive and negative ways of dealing with their own emotions. They also used their knowledge of how they were raised to be alert to their vulnerabilities as fathers. They realized that although their fathers had given them certain strengths, they also had passed on certain weaknesses, and they needed to watch for these weaknesses and make sure that they didn't create fatal flaws in their fathering approaches. By coming to terms with their pasts and gaining knowledge about how to parent in the present, both became excellent fathers.

The Benefits: Who This Book Is for and How It Will Help

Both Mike and Sam are traditional fathers, at least in the sense that they are married to and living with the mothers of their children. While it's great if you are in this traditional role, the lessons of this book apply to a wider range of fathers. You may be a stepfather, a divorced father living apart from your wife and child, the father of an adopted child, or some other variation on the traditional theme. As long as you are the primary father figure in a boy's life, everything in this book applies to you. Many men who aren't living with their sons or who aren't the biological parents feel that their influence is somehow diminished. It's not. Every boy needs a man who is emotionally and actively involved in his life. The involvement, support, and love he gives makes all the difference not only in their relationship but also in the type of man the boy becomes. As long as you are the main man in his life, what you do counts.

I've also written this book for fathers with sons of all ages. It's great if you read this book before your son is born and you are cognizant of all the issues before you start becoming a father. Prevention is worth an ounce of cure. Realistically, however, many of you will grab this book when you are experiencing doubts or problems as a father. This is fine, too, in that you can apply these ideas at any point and find that they will be relevant. I also want to stress that these topics are relevant no matter what type of problems you are having. It doesn't matter whether your boy is hyperactive, acting out, withdrawn, or constantly arguing with you. I'm not suggesting that this book will cure whatever ails the father-son relationship. Therapy may be necessary in some instances, and there may be situations where a son needs to be treated with medication. Nonetheless, I think most of you will find that you can put these ideas to practical use.

The benefits of this book are threefold. First, it's designed to improve the father-son relationship. When this relationship deteriorates, it's like a knife to the heart of a father. The anger, bitterness, and distance that come between dads and their boys are terrible things, and in the vast majority of cases, they can be avoided or remedied. Relationship breaks can occur as early as the preteen years, but they are especially common in adolescence and young adulthood. Much of what you will find in the following pages provides ways to repair and strengthen these relationships.

The second benefit is helping you raise a values-conscious boy who leads a happy, successful, and meaningful life. This is an ambitious goal, but fathers are in the best position to help their sons to realize this goal. What you do as a father in every developmental stage has a bearing on your son's future life. Many of my suggestions are geared toward increasing the odds that he will enjoy a terrific life. They are also designed to help him to become a terrific father to his own sons.

The third benefit is empowering you as a father. Too often, men feel helpless and hopeless as they attempt to deal with the challenges of raising boys. They are confused about what their roles and responsibilities are, about when they are doing too much and when they are doing too little. I can't promise you that this book will make fatherhood smooth sailing or that there won't be times when your son drives you a little bit crazy. I can tell you, however, that what you read here will provide you with a sense of your strength and impact as a father and how to use that strength to benefit the relationship.

As you probably can tell from what I have written here, this topic is of more than academic interest to me. I would like to tell you a little bit about my motivation for writing this book.

A Personal and a Professional Calling

Over the past 25 years, I have observed a growing crisis in father-son relationships first as a policeman, then as a high school counselor, and finally as a psychologist. From a purely social perspective, what I have witnessed is scary. As a policeman, I saw many boys who broke the law—murderers, dope dealers, gang members, and other criminals—and the overwhelming number of them came from fatherless homes. The tragedy of all these lost boys becoming amoral lawbreakers cannot be overstated. Anyone who spends time in law enforcement will tell you about the connection between absent fathers and boys' criminal behavior.

As a high school counselor and as a psychologist, I have worked with thousands of boys and their fathers, dealing with a more subtle form of abandonment and abuse. Many of the fathers I have counseled did not desert the family or beat their boys, but they inflicted a great deal of pain that left significant behavioral problems nonetheless. I have tried to help boys who were socially inept, bullies, hyperactive, experimenting with drugs and sex, and acting in other unacceptable ways. In just about every case their fathers' attitudes and actions had a profound influence on them. More significantly, the way to repair whatever damage had been done and help these boys lead normal, emotionally healthy lives required the involvement of their fathers. Over the years I have worked with thousands of fathers and sons, and many of the techniques I have used in my practice can be found in this book.

As much as I see a need for this book for social and professional reasons, I am also compelled to write it from a personal standpoint. I was 15 years old when my father moved out of the house, leaving my mother brokenhearted over the separation. For the entire summer, or so it seemed, my mother cried. Although I was relieved that this separation meant an end to their bitter fighting, I also was depressed that summer.

I always loved my father and had a soft spot for him. He was an immigrant and didn't fully understand the American way of sports or culture. Yet he did a pretty fair job of raising my sister and me. I always longed for his time, attention, and support. My father was a typical father of his era, soft-spoken, emotionally distant, hard working, uninvolved in the family day-to-day functioning, and rather heavy-handed when he was angry. My father cared about me, but it didn't much matter when I was a teenager. From that point until 10 years later, we hardly spoke. Because I didn't have a close relationship with my father, I felt lonely and isolated during those years.

Fortunately, two men entered my life who served as surrogate fathers. They lived on my block when I was growing up and took me under their wings. Dave Lehr and Mike Jones saved my life. These two guys were tough, smart, loving, and knew I needed a father more than I did. I would not be here writing this book or be a successful father if it hadn't been for these two men. They yelled at me for drinking, messing up at school, and being rude to my mother. They also gave me clear limits.

I learned firsthand that boys don't thrive without their father or a father figure in their life. I was lucky, and I knew it. These two men showed that fathering was a whole lot more than biology. These two men shaped me into a man and saved me from the perils of a fatherless childhood.

I hope to save others with this book. Or rather, I want to help other fathers save their sons by convincing them that fathering is a "calling" and not a part-time job or something that can be approached casually and effortlessly. Fathering requires everything a man can give to his son. If you make this commitment, you and your son will reap the benefits for the rest of your lives. As you start this book and assess how you're doing as a father, don't be discouraged no matter where you are falling short or how problematic your father-son relationship might be. Trust that you have the power to forge a strong, healthy relationship and that above all else, fathers matter.

Author's Note

All of the stories and voices contained in this book are derived in part from my clinical experience, research, law enforcement career, and my ministry experience. However, the names, places, and other details found in this book have been altered to protect the privacy and anonymity of the individuals to whom they refer. Therefore, any similarity between the names and stories of the individuals and families described in this book and those individuals known to readers is inadvertent and purely coincidental.

The use of masculine pronouns and specific reference to only fathers in this book are for the sole purpose of explaining the issues of fathers and sons. The apparent exclusion of feminine pronouns is for the purpose of writing, educating, and illustrating the subject matter only. The importance and relevance of mothers to this topic is covered.

Father
Your Son

1

The Power of Fathers

How to Empower the Relationship Rather than Just Yourself

I wish it didn't make such a difference, but I think my relationship with my dad was more important than I ever gave it credit for. I still occasionally think about him and wonder how things could have been better. No relationship has had more of a lasting effect on me than my father. I have spent the last 50 years proving him wrong in one way or another.

Dave, age 55

IF YOU DOUBT THIS statement, try an experiment. If your father has already died, recall how you felt when you first heard the news and in the weeks following his death. If your father is still alive, imagine receiving that terrible phone call informing you of his death.

When men talk to me about the death of their father, even the ones who maintain that they didn't have a close relationship say that they were surprised by how much it affected them. People routinely use terms such as *devastating* and *overwhelming* to describe their reactions. It is not unusual for men to suffer from depression or a period of questioning life's meaning and their own purpose following their father's death.

I guarantee that if you were to die, your son would be similarly affected. By then, of course, it's too late for you to do anything about it. Now is your opportunity. Even though it may not seem like it at times, your son pays close attention to your words and actions. What you say and do shapes his values, career decisions, and adult relationships. Even more significant, your "way" of being a father to your son determines if you enjoy a rich, rewarding relationship that you both relish or a poor, unsatisfying one filled with discomfort and tension.

You can make the right choice now or regret the wrong one for years to come. Every day I see fathers who beat themselves up over their lack of involvement and interest in their sons' lives when they were younger. Rick, for instance, told me how when his son was little he spent a great deal of time in the office and on the road, rationalizing that he was sacrificing for his family. With hindsight, Rick realized that he ran from the responsibility of being a father because he felt much more confident managing his direct reports than raising his son. "One of the worst things my son ever told me was when he was a teenager and we were having one of our many battles. He said, 'You know what you've taught me? All the things not to do when I become a father.'"

You don't have to become Rick. You can learn to use your power as a father consciously and effectively. I am going to disabuse you of misconceptions that often stand in the way of becoming a good father. I am going to provide you with the knowledge and tools you will need to fulfill this role effectively.

I am also not going to let you forget that fathers matter. They are needed in their sons' lives as much as mothers are needed in their daughters' lives. Same-sex parent identification helps both boys and girls develop a proper perspective of their role in the world.

The best fathers give their sons advice, structure, and love. Their eagerness and ability to be involved in their sons' lives and to develop emotionally intimate connections with them seal a bond that lasts a lifetime. They are types of fathers most sons dream about but never have. Instead, they end up with nightmare fathers who misuse their inherent power.

The Absent or Abusive Father

Fathers can be absent or abusive in many ways and thus misuse their power. Perhaps the most common category of absence is *physical*. Typically, physically absent fathers are divorced from the child's mom, although some may be workaholics and be at the office or on the road for long stretches. While some divorced fathers learn how to foster intimacy and involvement in their son's life despite the physical separation, many become defeated by the separation and "give up." They drift away from their sons because they believe the divorce has robbed them of their power.

Jack labored under this illusion. The father of five-year-old Marcus, he and his wife, Theresa, divorced when Marcus was three. Theresa subsequently remarried, and although Jack had regular visitations with Marcus, he began to feel that Marcus was no longer as attached to him as he once was. On more than one occasion Marcus called Theresa's new husband, "Daddy." Even though Theresa corrected Marcus and said that Jack was his father, Jack felt diminished as a parent. After a while, Jack began offering excuses about why he couldn't take Marcus during the weekend or cut short the time he spent with his son. When Jack was offered a job in another state, he didn't hesitate about taking it. After he moved, he saw Marcus only once or twice a year. In early adolescence, Marcus began to have trouble in school. Although he had a high IQ, he often didn't pay attention in class and talked back to teachers who corrected his mistakes. He also got into a number of fights with other students. Although Marcus had a good relationship with his stepfather, he clearly was angry about the lack of connection with his father, and his acting-out behaviors in school communicated this anger.

Fathers also can be *emotionally* absent. Again, the range of absentee behaviors runs the gamut. Some fathers are cold and distant. Others provide surface attention but do not connect with their child on a deeper level. Still others are only involved emotionally with their son in one area—sports is a common area of interest—but demonstrate little emotion in other aspects of a child's life.

Physically or verbally *abusive* fathers also can cause serious harm beyond the pain inflicted by a specific incident. Just about every family therapist has male patients who bear the scars of overly critical fathers. Not only can frequent tongue-lashings harm a boy's self-esteem and cause other developmental problems, but their negative effects can linger into adulthood, affecting everything from relationships to careers to life satisfaction. In addition, many of the boys who commit violent acts—from school shootings to gangbanging—come from homes where fathers were abusive or absent. As harmful as it is when there is no man in the home, it is even worse when the man who is there is abusive. When physical violence is the behavior being modeled by fathers, boys respond in kind, especially when they find someone weaker and more vulnerable than themselves.

Later I'll examine these negative consequences in more detail. For now, recognize that absence or abuse is not an option if you want to foster an emotionally healthy, mutually rewarding father-son relationship.

The Depth of Involvement: Going Beyond Token Participation

Most fathers tell me that they are involved in their sons' lives, and to a certain extent, they are correct. They attend their Little League games, take them out for pizza, and go on summer vacations with them. This type of involvement is good, but it is purely activity-based. Involvement should go beyond the surface, reaching the emotional core of boys. Sons of all ages need their fathers' guidance, support, and approval, and they won't receive these things without their fathers' commitment of time and emotional energy.

This isn't going to happen if you just show up. It takes real communication—talking honestly about your feelings and listening deeply to your son as he expresses his feelings. Being around and available is great, but you have to demonstrate that you care about what your son is doing, thinking, and feeling. Kids are sharp; they can tell if you're just going through the motions. They know if your body is there but your mind is a million miles away. Involvement takes effort. The challenge for fathers is to get beyond the inherent boredom of a fourth-grade piano recital and interact with a child on his level. Allowing him to express his concerns about the piece he's playing and complimenting him on the specific way he played it communicate your involvement; they reveal how much you support and approve of his efforts.

Fathers who are deeply involved in their sons' lives give them the gift of connection. No matter how uncertain and confusing their outer lives may be, these boys know that they are not alone. This recognition allows them to explore, grow, and develop rather than take few risks and remain stuck in a developmental stage. Boys who are connected to their fathers recognize that no matter how badly they mess up or how many times they fail, they can always count on their fathers' support.

This provides them with great resiliency both as children and as adults. Given all this, it is amazing that any father would miss the chance to be deeply involved in his son's life. Yet more often than not this involvement is missing or inconsistent.

The movie industry every year comes out with several movies that depict the emotional toll caused by uninvolved fathers. All these movies underscore the powerful need that both a father and a son have to reconnect and be resolved with each other despite past misunderstandings. In *My Life As a House*, for instance, Kevin Kline plays a character who has lost touch with his son, and the pain of this disconnection is amplified when he is diagnosed with a terminal disease. A number of scenes demonstrate how Kline's lack of involvement hurt his son when he was growing up and how Kline at last has recognized how much it has hurt him. Despite all the anger the son feels, each character is able to make an extraordinary effort to reconnect.

If art reflects life, why do so many fathers fail to forge strong connections with their sons? To answer the question, think about your own life. Your father may have been neglected by his father (sins of the father passed on to the son), and it appeared that he didn't matter to his father. We are all wired genetically, environmentally, and psychologically to expect that our father will love us. When this expectation is not met, we are devastated. Men generally ignore and minimize this emotional injury, putting up a tough front while inside the wound remains open and subject to infection. During our childhood and teen years, we become developmentally sidetracked and unable to form the deep and fulfilling relationships we crave.

If we do not understand our past, we are condemned to repeat it. Like father, like son is an unfortunate truism is this case. It seems natural to father our sons like we were fathered. We feel comfortable taking on this familiar parental role. It would feel unnatural and uncomfortable to take on a more connected role because such a parenting approach was never modeled for us. Therefore, we persist in being the type of father that, if we were to think long and hard about it, we don't want to be.

Are you less involved in your son's life than you should be? To assess your involvement, reflect on your answers to the following questions:

- When you have to choose between something you enjoy doing and attending an event involving your son, what choice do you usually make?

- When you go to an event involving your son that you are not particularly interested in, do you tend to zone out?
- When you spend a sustained period of time with your son, do you talk about what you are experiencing on a purely "intellectual" level or do you share feelings?
- Do you spend a significant, consistent amount of time with your son weekly, or is it insignificant and inconsistent?
- Do you offer your son support and approval when you are with your son, or are you generally neutral or disapproving?
- Do you use work as an excuse to avoid doing things with your son that don't particularly interest you?

Your answers will give you a rough measurement of your involvement. If you are like most fathers, you have some involvement deficiencies. To help yourself become aware of these deficiencies and take action to correct them, do the following exercise:

Focus on a childhood experience when you participated in a meaningful activity. Many people respond to this exercise by noting a triumphant moment in an athletic contest or a ceremony in which they received a reward. Whatever it is, search your memory for any situation like this in which your father was absent. Recall how you felt at the time. Write a short paragraph describing your sadness, anger, or whatever feelings you were experiencing. Then write a short paragraph describing how you would have felt if your father had been there.

Keep these two paragraphs in your wallet or in some other accessible place. Look at them frequently. They will remind you why your involvement in your son's life is so important and also serve as a warning about the powerful negative consequences when you are absent.

Embracing Intimacy: Real Men Develop Relationships

Men crave intimacy, although wives and children may dispute this point. Women often complain that their boyfriends or husbands have been "emotionally neutered" and that man-to-man conversations are all about sports and other surface issues. Sons may not complain out loud that their fathers refuse to share their feelings, but they wish that they were willing to do so. Boys have a natural need to tell their fathers that they are disappointed, angry, happy, excited, or ashamed, but they often adopt the stoic model of their fathers. For many fathers their parenting style isn't all that different from their managerial style at work. They are authoritative, reasonable, and intelligent in their decisions, but they don't let their feelings show, fearful of appearing vulnerable. Deep down, they want an emotionally intimate relationship with their sons, but they are paying for the relationship their father had with them.

Men often have trouble with intimacy because they were emotionally crushed when they attempted to form an intimate bond with their own fathers. Intimate relationships become high-risk endeavors for men who have little positive emotional experience or connection with their fathers. For these men, sharing a fear or vulnerability with a son feels as scary as skydiving for the first time or any other type of risky activity. To them, exposing their deepest feelings is a betrayal of their own fathers, and they don't want to betray them. They were taught in early developmental stages by their fathers to be strong and guard their weaknesses. They were reprimanded if they cried when they scraped their knees and were told not to act like a "baby" or a "sissy." This code of conduct was drilled into their psyches, and to show their feelings to their son feels like a betrayal of this code.

Duncan's father, for instance, was a banker who was kind and considerate to his wife and open and emotional with his daughters. With Duncan, however, he generally was reserved and rarely offered support or approval. He wanted to raise Duncan to be "tough" in part because his own father had raised him that way and it had helped him get through adolescence living in a tough neighborhood. Even though Duncan's father was making a good living and the family lived in a middle-class neighborhood, he wanted to be sure that bullies didn't pick on his son. For this reason, he was tough with Duncan, chastising him when he cried, even when Duncan was a young boy. Although Duncan's father would express his sadness, joy, and other emotions when interacting with Duncan's sisters, he would reign in these feelings when communicating with Duncan. Once Duncan was crestfallen when he failed to be named the quarterback on his Peewee football team, and he told his father how upset he was and that he felt that the decision wasn't fair. Duncan still remembers what his father said: "Life isn't fair, so get used to it."

As an adult, Duncan married, and he and his wife had two children, the oldest of whom was a boy. Duncan felt that he was raising his son differently than his father had raised him. For one thing, he was not as strict as his father was and didn't try to make his son tough. He also didn't yell at him as his father had yelled at him when he made a mistake or complained. Duncan, though, found it difficult to communicate openly and honestly with his son. It wasn't as if Duncan were consciously holding back his emotions, but he generally didn't show much joy or excitement when his son told him about an accomplishment, and he gently (but skillfully) dissuaded his son from expressing his fears or other strong emotions. In these situations, Duncan would distract his son from these emotional expressions by making him laugh, using sarcasm or other techniques to turn his son's feelings into a joke. While Duncan may have succeeded in distracting his son from his troubling feelings, he also created an emotional gap in the relationship that invariably will cause his son problems in the coming years.

Do you have an emotionally intimate relationship with your son? Or are you abusing the power of the relationship by withholding your feelings? To assess the intimacy of the relationship, think about how you would answer the following questions:

- Have you ever cried in front of your son? Do you allow yourself to show your sadness in front of him, or do you hide it from him?
- When your son is angry, hurt, or fearful, do you encourage him to express his negative feelings and explore them in conversation with you?
- If your son has a problem with another kid at school or is experiencing feelings that make you uncomfortable, are you likely to hand off the problem to your wife?
- When you talk with your son about activities and events that are important to him, do you allow him to express how he feels about these activities and events (or do you steer the conversation toward the specifics of what happened)?
- Can you recall any conversation with your son in the past year in which you told him you were disappointed or upset about something in your own life?

It's not uncommon for men to look at these questions and respond defensively. To them, the questions suggest weakness. Crying in front of their sons feels "wrong," a violation of their macho code. Similarly, they assume that asking their boys to express their hurts and fears encourages whining and weakness. You may find that you're responding defensively, and this type of response can prevent you from really thinking about the questions and answering honestly. Therefore, try to suspend your defensive reaction for the moment and analyze your behaviors objectively relative to each question.

If your answers suggest emotional intimacy is a problem for you, then you need to work on understanding your relationship with your own father. There is a freedom that comes from knowing and accepting your father. Once you grasp what made your father tick and work through your feelings about it, this insight will liberate the artificial constraints you have placed on your feelings. Free from the unconscious code of conduct your father taught you, you can act toward your son in a much more emotionally honest manner. Too often we deny our feelings about our fathers or never come to terms with the legacy we inherited from them. We may think that we are not affected by our fathers' child-raising approach, but what we often do not realize is that sons are.

Admittedly, this type of understanding does not happen overnight. In the following chapters I will provide a variety of information and tools that will help you to come to terms with who your father was and how his attitudes and behaviors affected you. For now, though, let's start off with a simple exercise that will help you to think of your father in ways you may not have considered before.

Pretend that you are a reporter for a tabloid newspaper assigned to write a provocative profile of a celebrity, who happens to be your father. Your goal is to reveal the man beneath the public celebrity, to expose the motivations and dreams of the individual who no one really knows beyond his public persona. Have fun with the profile; create a headline; be controversial. You might start the profile like this: "John Doe grew up as the only child of a steelworker, and some say molten metal flows through his veins rather than blood." The point of this exercise is to get you to look at your father from another angle than the one with which you usually view him. Put on your reporter's hat and start writing.

The Conscious Father

Being involved and emotionally intimate as a father does not mean turning yourself into Mr. Softy or "feminizing" your fathering approach. Instead, your goal is to achieve a balance of compassion, insight, strength, and flexibility. This is almost impossible to do if you parent in a daze. Too often men believe that being a father is as natural as walking. In fact, it is about as natural as hitting a golf ball into a tiny hole from a great distance. Being a father to a son, like golfing, is a learned art that requires an acute awareness of all the little things that go into the process. Compassion, insight, strength, and flexibility are the natural result of being a highly conscious father. Paying attention to your relationship with your father and his relationship with his father is part of this consciousness. Taking the time and developing the perception to understand what your son is feeling are also part of this awareness. Listening to feedback you receive from your wife, your children, and others is another way to become a conscious father.

Some men disdain conscious parenting of their sons because they cede this responsibility to their wives. I cannot overemphasize what a mistake this is. It is not that women do not play an important role in their sons' development. It is simply that a mother, no matter how caring and skilled she is at being a mother, cannot fully substitute for a father. Single mothers often are forced to be both mother and father to their children, but they just as often do a better job with their daughters than with their sons.

Cindy is a divorced mother, and I have been working with her and her son, Connor. Cindy recently was in my office to discuss why sports are so important to her son. She told me, "I always have a pain in my heart when I have to play catch with Connor and he tells me not to throw the ball like a girl. I tell him I am a girl, and his face always looks sad when I say that. There is always a gap for him with other boys because I can't be his father." Connor is also keenly aware of his mother's limitations and the absent father in his life. Connor's father refuses to see him until Cindy reduces the child support he has to pay. Although Connor is stoic about his father's absence from his life, a significant psychological toll is being exacted. Connor will have to work very hard in his adult years to overcome this negative picture of his father and men in general. It will be very difficult for Connor to embrace his masculinity with such a damaged image of his father, who on a psychological level represents all men. In fact, he will be lucky if he doesn't grow up to be an angry young man, an all too common fate of boys without fathers.

I relate this story not just to criticize fathers who are physically absent but also to warn all fathers about the dangers of distancing themselves from their sons. When men are emotionally absent—when they are unconscious fathers—they do psychological damage to their sons. In the 1950s, psychologist Robert Sears, a developmental specialist, and his colleagues examined the child-rearing practices of more than 300 American parents when their children were five years old. Twenty-six years later, another group of researchers evaluated these young adults from the original study to assess their level of empathy and compare it with Sears's original findings. The researchers found that the most powerful predictor of empathy in adulthood was paternal child-rearing involvement at age five. This factor proved to be a better predictor than several maternal predictors and was equally evident for boys and girls.

In a third follow-up study of this original group, these children were now 41 years of age. The adults who reported having satisfying, fulfilling social relationships in midlife—having a long, happy marriage, having children, engaging in recreational activities with others outside the family—were the ones who had experienced more paternal warmth during childhood. These studies clearly point to the invaluable roles fathers have in the family and with their sons' long-term development.

While these studies identify the benefit of conscious fathering, they do not have much impact on most men. Fortunately, the men's movement has done a good job of raising men's consciousness. The men's movement is roughly at the same point that the women's movement was at 30 years ago. The process is just beginning, but already we are seeing men who are expanding their role as father beyond the traditional one of provider. They recognize that the 1950s "father knows best" approach is an anachronism, that they have to move beyond the notion of father as dispenser of wisdom from on high. Rather than take the responsibility of being a father for granted, men need to open their eyes and their minds to what this responsibility really entails. The following consciousness-raising exercise will provide a good start toward achieving this goal.

True or False: Learning the Truth About Father-Son Relationships Can Help You Become a Better Father

Myths and misconceptions about fatherhood often prevent men from developing the awareness necessary for good parenting. As I have suggested, men subscribe to all sorts of myths and misconceptions. To banish them, the first truth every man should keep in mind is this: *Fathers matter.* It is impossible to overestimate the impact of dads on their sons' development through adulthood, their happiness and success as adults, and their ability to be good fathers when they have sons.

The following true-false quiz will enable you get a sense of how much you know about being a father to your son. If you find yourself getting answers wrong, don't be discouraged. Most fathers never took a course in parenting and especially were never taught how to be fathers to their sons. The rest of this book will help you to pass this fathering test with flying colors.

True or False

1. Fathers and mothers serve basically the same role in raising boys.
2. Sons learn how to be assertive and confident from their fathers and emotional intelligence from their mothers.
3. Biological fathers have a much greater influence on their sons than stepfathers or other nonbiological father figures.
4. Men can overcome a fatherless past.
5. Fathers affect their sons for their entire lives.
6. Teenage boys do not need their fathers as much as toddlers do.
7. It is impossible for men to learn anything from fathers they hated.
8. Not all boys crave a positive father-son relationship.
9. The wounds men suffer as sons prevent them from being good fathers.
10. Many boys do not pay much attention to their fathers.
11. While men should avoid any physical abuse of their sons, a certain amount of verbal abuse is a natural part of a father-son relationship.
12. Most boys are affected by tension between fathers and mothers.

Answers

1. *False.* Fathers serve as role models for their sons just as mothers serve as role models for their daughters. Although mothers can provide their sons with strong support and help them to develop good values, they cannot pretend to be something they are not. For instance, a son's ability to be a good husband and father is directly related to his relationship with his own father as he is growing up.

2. *False.* The three primary emotions are love, sadness, and anger, and the more a father is able to communicate these emotions to his son in a healthy way, the more the son will be able to develop emotional intelligence.

3. *False.* Fathering is beyond biology. In fact, *stepfather* is a legal term, not a relational one. If you are the primary male figure in a boy's life, you are the one who will have the greatest influence over him and how he develops.

4. *True.* Not having a father or having a horrible relationship with him does not sentence you to repeat the past with your own son. You can make the necessary changes in yourself to give your son what you never received from your father. Of course, making these changes means making a commitment to being a present, conscious father.

5. *True.* Even after you die, your son will be affected by your relationship with him. No matter what boys say to their fathers— for example, "I'll never be like you"—or how much they try to distance themselves as adolescents, they are profoundly affected by who you are and how you interacted with them.

6. *False.* It just appears that teenagers don't need their fathers. In reality, they have an inherent desire for a strong relationship.

7. *False.* In therapy, men can get past their hatred for their fathers and learn from them. Analyzing the father-son relationship can yield many insights that will help sons to make positive adjustments to their life and help them to become better fathers.

8. *False.* At times, some boys seem as if they do not need their fathers, especially in the wake of a bitter divorce. There are also boys who appear to be so independent or so close to their mothers that they create the illusion that a relationship with

their father is of no consequence. In reality, every son seeks and requires this relationship.

9. *False.* Growing up with a conflicted, abusive father is not a reason to repeat the sins of the past or become convinced that you are doomed to be a failure as a father. I have seen many sons of tyrannical and even seriously disturbed men become terrific fathers, primarily because they addressed their emotional wounds rather than deny them or pretend they weren't as serious as they were.

10. *False.* Boys watch their fathers like hawks, although they also may have developed the skill of watching them surreptitiously. Boys are highly sensitized to even the nuances of a father's words and actions, and even a small facial tic of approval or disapproval is magnified from their perspective.

11. *False.* In some ways, cruel words cut deeper than physical blows. Abusive behavior is the inability to communicate your feelings with words in a constructive manner. While every father loses his temper with his son on occasion, verbal abuse goes beyond simple anger and is designed to inflict pain.

12. *True.* A major misconception is that only divorce causes psychological damage to children. In fact, tension and conflict over the long term can be even more harmful to kids than a divorce.

Separating fact from fiction can help you to become a better father to your son. Knowledge can be a powerful ally in your quest to form a stronger relationship with him, which is why the next step involves exploring your past and getting to know your father in ways you never knew him as a child.

2

Discovering Your Father for Your Son's Sake

I remember holding the screen door open as my father carried his stuff to the car. I was seven, and I knew it was a bad day. He never lived with us again. Even though I saw him after he left, it was never the same. We all died that day, and we still don't talk about it.

Tony, age 44

I haven't seen my dad in over 28 years. My parents divorced when I was 14 years old, and my mom moved to Los Angeles from New York. I went to live with my dad when I was 15 for a year. I moved back when we had a discussion that I had to pick him or my mother. I didn't want to do that, so he told me to go live with my mother. We haven't spoken since 1975. It's taken me a long time to recover from that discussion with my father. It really broke my heart then and still does.

Gregg, age 43

W E WOULD BE MUCH better fathers to our sons if we had a much better understanding of our own fathers. If you are like most men, though, you find the subject painful. You don't want to talk to your spouse, friends, or children about how your father made you feel when you were growing up. You don't want to analyze your father's behaviors toward you and how they influenced the person you became.

This is true even if you didn't experience a traumatic incident involving your father, as Gregg and Tony did. Think about the last time you opened up to someone about your father. This doesn't mean telling someone what a great athlete your father was or mentioning that you inherited his bad back. When did you last have an in-depth discussion involving your feelings about your father? At best, you probably can count these discussions on the fingers of one hand. At worst, you can't recall this type of conversation at all.

Men's reluctance to explore these issues isn't always because their fathers physically or verbally abused them or because their parents' divorce hurt them. Instead, men "naturally" avoid intense, life-shaping feelings from their childhood. It may not be a specific incident but a pattern of paternal behavior that made them feel ashamed, scared, or angry. They don't want to think about all those times their father didn't acknowledge their achievements or contributed to their sense of insecurity or inferiority. Men also don't want to focus on how what happened all those years ago affects their own fathering behaviors. It is scary to realize that you are having the same negative impact on your son as your father had on you. While your behaviors around your son are probably different, you are conjuring up the same feelings in him.

Exploring these feelings, however, can make you a much more "conscious" father and help you to change your behaviors toward your son in a positive way. Men father reflexively. They don't think a lot about what they are going to say to their sons at any given moment or how their actions may affect their sons. As a result, they slip into patterns that are directly related to their experiences with their own fathers, and some of these patterns are not emotionally healthy.

Before we start this exploration process, I want to be clear on one thing: This isn't about blaming your father. Even the best fathers in the universe make mistakes. You are not going to be a better father to your son by scapegoating your dad. Instead, the key is to explore the emotional impact of the relationship and to apply the lessons learned to your own role as a father. Remember, you can't heal what you don't acknowledge.

The Illusion of Protection

You are never going to be willing to examine your relationship with your father until you stop protecting him—and yourself. Subconsciously, you are terrified of what would happen if the details of this relationship were exposed. Even if nothing truly terrible happened during your developmental years, it *feels* terrible. When you are a five-year-old whose father snubs him, it seems like a slap in the face. You may have been raised in an environment of numerous arguments, and the memory of all the then-traumatic fights still feels traumatic now, even though they were typical family fare. From your perspective, it seems pointless to expose these feelings to scrutiny. The possibility of re-creating these youthful arguments and feelings of rejection and embarrassment is nil, but in the back of your mind you don't want to take the chance. The pain of those early experiences subconsciously subverts logical analysis.

It is also possible that you and your father did have major problems—he was physically or emotionally absent or physically or verbally abusive—but you have managed to patch things up as adults and get along reasonably well. As a result, you want to protect the decent relationship you have forged. For instance, Robert's father was a borderline sadist. Robert recalls his dad beating him as well as verbally assaulting him until he cried. Robert will only grudgingly admit these facts, however. He refuses to delve into his feelings about these experiences, saying with a mixture of resignation and anger, "What is done is done." Robert, though, is experiencing serious problems with his own son. Although he is not abusive in the way that his father was, he is very distant. He rarely attends his son's Little League games, and when he is with his son, Robert infrequently initiates conversation. It is almost as if he is afraid to become close, convinced that such intimacy will unleash his anger. Robert also wants to protect his father, who is now elderly and in poor health. Although Robert doesn't realize it, he is protecting his father from his own anger that would bubble to the surface if he dug into the events of his childhood.

You may be reacting to the preceding paragraph by saying to yourself, "This isn't me." You may be convinced that you are not protecting anyone; you simply don't want to dredge up the past. Consider, though, whether this subject makes you anxious. Anxiety is a fear-based emotion related to the feeling of uncertainty and the need for emotional safety. Your father's unpredictable behavior, an unstable home life, abuse in all forms, alcoholism, and many other scary childhood situations could have produced this anxiety. You became hypervigilant in response to this anxiety, a perfectly normal reaction. Emotional vigilance is an attempt to feel safe when living in what feels like a chaotic situation. Children as young as three years old learn how to be emotionally vigilant, protecting themselves from feeling overwhelmed, helpless, hopeless, and hurt. The purpose of this vigilance is control. If they are constantly on guard, they feel more in control of their environment. The problem, of course, is that these controlling children can grow up to become controlling adults—and controlling fathers.

It may seem to you that controlling your memories and your articulation of them protects you from childhood anxiety. This is an illusion. You are merely repressing the anxiety, and if you don't deal with it, it will grow in intensity and scope and come back to haunt both you and your son. Dealing with this anxiety means exploring your relationship with your father as if it were a cave. It's dark, it's scary, and it's uncertain where it leads. Fortunately, you have a guide who will equip you for a safe and productive "spelunking" expedition.

Digging Deep: It's Scary in the Dark

The "cave" is nothing more than that place inside us where taboo feelings reside. We may not "see" these feelings clearly, but when they emerge, we have a sense of danger and dread. As in a cave, we have gone beneath the surface and are encountering things that are usually left in the dark. To get a sense of what it's like to be there, do the following:

1. Recall a major emotional trauma from your past. It doesn't have to be about your father, but it should be some incident that hit you hard. For instance, it could be a phone call in the middle of the night informing you of a loved one's death; a doctor's diagnosis that begins, "I'm afraid I have some bad news"; someone you care about dumping you; or your boss telling you that you've been let go from a job you love.
2. Try to write a paragraph describing how you felt at that moment.
3. Reflect on how long you experienced these feelings. In other words, did these feelings dominate your thoughts for a minute, a day, a week, a month, or more?
4. Determine if these feelings dissipated on their own or if you forcibly separated yourself from them.
5. Think about how and why you ran from these feelings.

The goal of this exercise is to help you to become more familiar with the cave state. Its unfamiliarity caused you to flee from it prematurely. Rather than confront the feelings you encountered, you turned your back on them. Some of you will recall the conscious act of "pulling yourself together" and refusing to "feel bad" any longer. You may remember giving yourself an excuse to leave the cave—you needed to focus on work, on your children, or on getting on with your life. You also may recall that that you limited your stay in this dark place to a relatively short period of time, fearing that if you allowed it to go on, it might consume you.

The good news is that we are built tough. Most of us are tremendously resilient, and we are able to enter this cave of scary feelings and emerge unscathed. In fact, if you think about it, you have visited this cave a number of times in response to something your father did or said. For instance, you realized that you didn't have a father like all the other boys at school when he was the only dad who didn't attend his kids' Little League games. For a little while, you plunged into the cave but quickly extricated yourself. As an active boy rather than a reflective man, you intuitively understood that this wasn't an appropriate place for you. As an adolescent and young adult, though, you could investigate the dark emotions relating to your father, but you probably were too angry to do so. If you had an absent or abusive father, you are probably too defensive, resentful, and hostile to engage in this exploration on your own. Just think back to your adolescent feelings toward your father, and you can taste that anger. Think about all the times he didn't show up when he promised he would be there. Remember all the put-downs and cutting remarks. Recall how much it hurt, and that anger will quickly come bubbling to the surface.

You need to explore these feelings so that they won't taint your relationship with your son. In therapy, we usually take some easy, tentative steps so that people can become acclimated to the environment. Let's focus on how you can take these first steps into the cave.

Entering the Cave

Start out looking for an old memory. Imagine a cave that contains these memories, but they are not in plain sight. Instead, they are secreted in hidden parts of the cave, obscured by shadow. This is fortunate because if everything were well illuminated, all your childhood memories of your father would come rushing back and overwhelm you, and then you would certainly run from the cave. This way, though, you can examine one memory at a time.

Think back to something your father did that bothered you in some way. Don't choose an incident that was highly traumatic or that you remember with tremendous hurt. Instead, select an event that was only moderately painful. Maybe it was your father's unwillingness to give you a compliment when you finally received an A in a tough subject. Perhaps it was his insistence that you go hunting with him, even though you hated guns and shooting animals. Perhaps it was just his failure to show up at an important event in your life, such as a piano recital or an athletic contest.

Whatever it was, roll the memory around in your mind. Sit with it for a while. Refamiliarize yourself with exactly what took place. Begin with the specifics of the incident. If you would like, write a description of what took place. Or if there is someone with whom you feel comfortable—a spouse or a good friend—describe it to this person. Concentrate on the details rather than the emotions initially. If possible, look at it as if you were a newspaper reporter doing a story—or more in keeping with our metaphor, a spelunker finding an object in a cave.

The following is an example of a written description:

When I was eight or so, we visited friends in another state, and they had a tree house in their backyard. I thought it was the greatest thing in the world, and I asked my father if I could have one. He said that I was too young, but that if I wanted, it could be my birthday present when I was 10. For the next two years I occasionally asked my father if I could have a tree house yet, but he kept telling me I was too young. On the morning of my tenth birthday, though, I was sure that I would find a tree house in the crook of an old oak tree in our backyard. For some reason, I was convinced that my father was going to surprise me with this gift. I remember going out into the backyard first thing in the morning, but there was no tree house. When I asked my father about it, he shook his head and told me that he'd just been too busy to get around to build-

ing it, but maybe next year he'd have time. I remember opening my presents that morning and still expecting that a tree house would magically appear, that my father would say he wanted to surprise me and that it would be delivered whole to the house. I kept watching that tree for the tree house, not just on my birthday but for weeks afterward, certain that it would be there, but it never was.

Next, move on to how you felt about this incident. Start with a simple declaration of your emotional state, such as, "I felt sad" or "I felt angry." Don't focus on how you felt as much as on *describing* how you felt. You want to creep up on the emotion, as if it were hiding in a corner of the cave and you don't want to startle it—or it to startle you. Once you have captured it in a sentence, then try to remember the emotion in greater depth. Try to recapture the emotional ramifications by answering the following:

- On a scale of 1 to 10 (with 10 being the most), how angry, resentful, sad, or disappointed were you?
- Was this emotion directed more at your father than at yourself? If so, why?
- Did you ever articulate this emotion to your father? Did you ever tell him or show him how his behavior made you feel?
- How long did you feel this way? Was it a relatively short period of time, or did the feelings linger?

As you answer the questions, you probably will feel the feelings intensify. The shame, anger, fear, or whatever the emotion was becomes palpable. The wound that your father inflicted, whether intentional or not, still hurts, perhaps almost as much as the day you received it. When you were a child, it hurt to have a dream dashed or a hope mocked, and perhaps surprisingly, the wound hasn't healed. You can take heart, however, from the knowledge that this is the first step toward healing this wound. Rather than letting it reside in the recesses of your mind and do its damage to your father-son relationship without you being aware of it, you are bringing it out in the open. By doing so, you are reducing its power to influence your behaviors.

Going Deeper into the Cave

Now you are ready to journey to darker places. As scary as this may sound, you are much better prepared for this journey after taking the preceding step. You will find that you have gained an increased tolerance for the painful memories that you will uncover. To get at these memories, answer the following questions:

- To what degree was your father absent in your life when you were growing up? On a scale of 1 to 10 (with 10 indicating a constant presence), how would you rate the consistency with which he was there for you? Did your father's absence increase or decrease as you grew up? Did your relationship stay the same with your father most of your life?
- Can you recall a specific instance when you felt abandoned, neglected, or rejected? Do you remember a pattern of abandonment, neglect, or rejection from your childhood? When you recall that pattern and how it made you feel then, what words would you use to describe it? Thinking about it now, does it evoke the same feelings? Why do you think what you father did was so harmful?
- What was one of the scariest things that ever happened between you and your father? Why was it so scary? Was there physical violence? Did it involve screaming and saying things that were terribly hurtful? Did it seem like the incident created a "point of no return" for the relationship?
- When you hear your father's voice in your head, what is he saying to you? Is the voice critical of you? What common refrain from your childhood or adolescence do you hear?
- When you allow yourself to feel angry about something your father did to you when you were growing up, what is it that you are angry about? Is it one specific thing? Or is it a series of incidents? Think about why you were so angry with him and how or if you expressed that anger back then.
- What oaths or pledges did you make about being a father when you were growing up? Finish the following sentences: I swore that I would never _____. I promised myself to _____. It is really important to me that _____.
- What is one thing that you are ashamed of as your father's son?

Again, the goal is to answer these questions in writing or by talking with a trusted person in your life. You do not have to answer every single question but rather address the key issues in your past. You will know that you are addressing these issues if you experience the same emotions that you felt long ago. It is astonishing how long we can keep the intensity of our anger, resentment, or shame intact, and it is a testament to the power of a father over a son. Don't be afraid of these emotional responses. By thinking about them, expressing them, and feeling them, you will be helping yourself and your son.

To give you a sense of the form this expression can take, here's a portion of what Jake, a father of three boys, wrote:

I must have been 14 or 15 when my father packed up and left home, and that's when the scariest moment in our relationship occurred. Though I didn't know all the details at the time, he had been having an affair with a woman in his office, and my mother had kicked him out of the house. She literally threw his belongings out of the house, and I remember standing there hating him for what he had done and wanting him to apologize to my mother and try and work things out. When my mother had started throwing his stuff out, I ran outside because she was screaming at him, and I wanted to get away. But once I was outside, I just stood there. When my father came out, he tried to talk to me, but I was so confused and angry that when he apologized, I said, "I don't care." I remember how hurt he was and feeling horrible that I had hurt him that way but also glad because he deserved it. And then he told me not to worry, that he'd be seeing me again soon. I said, "I never want to see you again." I also started crying, which was incredibly embarrassing because a lot of the neighbors were out watching this scene unfold. At the time, I really believed that he had done something so awful and I had said something so awful that I never would see him again.

By articulating this emotional trauma, Jake doesn't guarantee that he won't inadvertently produce the same feelings of abandonment and loss in his own sons. He does, however, reduce the odds that he will have this negative impact just by taking these feelings out of the cave and dragging them into the light. Even if Jake does nothing else recommended in these pages, he will have made a positive impact on his father–son relationships.

Living in the Present

Once you have done these cave exercises, you are in a much better position to separate the past from the present. While you can do this easily enough intellectually, it is much more difficult to do emotionally, and this is where you run into trouble. For instance, let's say that your father was often indifferent to you, concentrating his attention on work and your mother. He didn't put in much floor time with you when you were a toddler, and his stoic demeanor prevented him from offering you much encouragement or even engaging you in many meaningful conversations. As a result, you grew up craving his approval and attention and resenting him for rarely giving it to you.

As an adult, this unsatisfied craving may result in a number of negative parenting behaviors. You may try to be attentive and encouraging in one area of your son's life where your father ignored you, but you inadvertently may be indifferent in other areas of your son's life—areas that are meaningful to him. You may overreact to your unexpressed feelings and overwhelm your son with attention, suffocating him with your intrusions into his life and not realizing when it is wise to back off.

Whatever negative parenting behaviors result, you now are sufficiently conscious of your feelings to separate past from present. You can diminish the reflexive word or act in response to buried emotions. When your son asks you to play catch, you don't start correcting everything from his throwing motion to the way he catches the ball. You are more aware that his request has triggered emotions from your childhood, when your father always had an excuse why he couldn't play catch with you, and that your overly intrusive behavior is a reaction to emotions raised 30 years ago.

To separate past from present, keep the following adage in mind:

You cannot let go of what you aren't holding.

In other words, it is impossible to let go of all the rage, shame, and resentment your father's parenting built up in you unless you take conscious hold of it. You can only let go of the past and live in the present when you "possess" all the things you discover in the cave. Only then can you react to your son in the present without the past intruding on how you speak to and act toward him.

If this sounds like psychological mumbo-jumbo, let me try to describe the process by which the past acts on the present. In our childhood, we experience trauma that is so overwhelming or painful that we cannot process it fully when we are young. To survive the trauma, we numb ourselves to the awful event and the feelings the event engenders. We need to restore sensation to these numbed pieces of our emotional memory. By doing so, we make ourselves whole. As a child, as an adolescent, and even as a young adult, we numbed ourselves to our father's attitudes and actions. As a wise adult and as a father, however, we no longer have this luxury. To be a good father, we need to be a whole father. Otherwise, we are parenting with one foot in the past.

To separate your past from your present, try this experiment: Recall a recent incident with your son in which you lost your temper or he became angry with you (or both). With this incident in mind, do the following:

1. Detail your response to your son. What specifically did you say or do?
2. Determine what your father would have done if he were in your situation. If, for instance, you son started whining about having to get dressed up to go out to dinner, how would your father have responded?
3. Specify how your father's response would have been different from your own. What would he have said or done that is different from how you responded?
4. Given these differences, do you see any underlying relationship between what your father would have done and what you did? Did you do the exact opposite of your father? Even though you and your father may take different approaches, is it likely that your actions would produce the same reaction in your son?

While you may not always be able to spot the relationship, this experiment trains you to watch for linkages between how your father parented you and how you parent your son. Being conscious of how he treated you will help you avoid reacting in the present to how he made you feel in the past. When you realize that he would have screamed at your son in a given situation and that you refused to raise your voice (even though your son did something worthy of a serious reprimand), you grasp that your response was motivated by something that happened years ago.

Bringing the Anger into the Open

Although it may not seem like it on the surface, your parenting behaviors with your son have been strongly influenced by your father's behaviors toward you. As much as you may consciously reject his parenting style, you are still under its sway. Most adult sons have tremendous amounts of unresolved anger involving their fathers, but this anger is often directed at other people besides their fathers. Typically, someone—usually a spouse or child—says or does something that triggers negative feelings similar to those catalyzed years ago by the father. Your son, for instance, may stubbornly refuse to go shopping for a baseball mitt with you, and subconsciously, you are reminded of how your father stubbornly refused to take you anywhere. As a result, you become unreasonably angry at your son's refusal, yelling at him and calling him selfish.

You need to deal with your anger toward your father to avoid or reduce these scenarios, and the way to do so is by recognizing that the anger is simply a smoke screen covering up the real injury your father inflicted, an injury that involves abandonment, neglect, or rejection. To help you to identify and talk about this anger, I have created a list of the most common things fathers say and do to anger their sons. I have arranged the lists based on the three categories of abandonment, neglect, and rejection. Review the list and check which ones apply to you:

Abandonment

_____ Physically leaving because of divorce or other marital problems

_____ Spending an inordinate amount of time in the office or on the road

_____ Spending a great deal of time with friends or pursuing interests rather than being with you at home

Neglect

_____ Paying little attention when you had something important to say

_____ Ignoring your requests for feedback or attendance at specific events

_____ Being unwilling to engage in meaningful conversations

Rejection

_____ Refusing to express his love for you

_____ Telling you to go away and stop bothering him (a pattern of rejection)

_____ Dismissing your ideas and feelings

These are obviously just a few of many examples. A list of reasons for feeling rejection would take up two or three pages alone. Use the handful of examples here to stimulate your own angry childhood memories involving your father. Again, thinking and talking about these memories is key. If you find it difficult to discuss them with a spouse or other trusted person in your life, try using the following technique:

Pretend that your father is in the room with you and that you have a chance to tell him about how angry you were with him when you were a child, teenager, or young adult. Don't blame him for what he did or use this exercise to "vent." Instead, your goal is to communicate your feelings with precision; you want him to understand exactly what he did that wounded you and why he caused you to experience abandonment, neglect, or rejection. Express to him

- How you felt
- Why you felt that way
- A specific incident that illustrates this feeling

Here is a sample expression:

When I was a child, you made me feel like I wasn't worthy of your attention because you always had your nose buried in the financial section of the paper when you were home or you locked yourself up in your office. I felt like I didn't really matter to you, or that I was far down on the list. I remember once I had an assignment from school in which we

*were supposed to interview our fathers about what they did for a living
and write a report, and you told me that it was a silly assignment, and
I had to get the information for the report from mom.*

Finally, the way to deal with this anger is to remind yourself that
your father's legacy to you was not all negative. This obvious point is
easy to forget, especially when you return to the cave and unearth all
the anger that resides there. Blaming your father for the "bad" things
he did and said will not help you to be a better father to your son. What
will help, though, is making peace with who he was. To this end,
answer the following questions about your father:

- What compliments do people give you that reflect traits or
  attitudes passed on to you by your father?
- What piece of advice did your father give you that has turned
  out to be valuable?
- What is the best day you remember having with your father
  during your childhood? What did he do or say that contributed
  to it being a great day?
- What were your father's strengths as a person? What was he
  particularly good at from professional or personal standpoints?
  What did you admire about him when you were a child?

Few men have fathers who were thoroughly evil or who were absolutely horrible fathers. Even if they were "bad" fathers in the relative
sense of the term, they probably had at least a few positive parenting
traits and you experienced some good times because of them. These
good memories, freshly revisited, can take some of the bitterness out of
your feelings toward your dad. Again, I'm not suggesting that you
whitewash the past or lie to yourself about who your father was.
Instead, you should make sure you are aware of both the good and bad
traits of your dad. Don't expect this awareness to happen overnight, but
returning to these exercises every so often will help you gradually to
dissipate some of the negative emotions you harbor.

There's another person in this equation, however, who we haven't
yet considered. Whether you knew or were close with your father's
father doesn't particular matter. What matters is understanding how
your father was parented. This understanding will unlock much of the
mystery of his fathering style and will give you greater freedom to parent
your own son in the present rather than in the past.

3

The Three-Generation Pattern
and How to Break It

My grandfather told me to never let my emotions run me—and that men don't cry. I have only cried two times in my life, and one of them was at his funeral. The other was when I caught my dad with our neighbor's wife. Men don't cry in my family.

Mark, age 37

I wish we could have gotten along better. Andy and I were never close and still aren't. I worked a lot, and his mother did what mothers did in those days, everything. We don't talk much now, and we are very similar to my father and myself. My father and I hardly spoke after I moved out of the house and went to Europe in World War II.

Ben, age 78

JUST AS WE NEED to be aware of our genetic heritage for medical reasons, we need to recognize the patterns and problems that are passed down from one father to the next. Realistically, most of us can't obtain much information about the men in our family beyond our grandfathers, although it would be useful to profile our great-grandfather and his father and grandfather. If we could see six or seven generations of fathers and examine their parenting behaviors with their sons, a clear pattern would quickly emerge.

This pattern would be extraordinarily useful to you as a father in that it would allow you to identify tendencies and traits that have been passed down through the generations and that might be harming your son. The most obvious generational fathering problem is physical abuse, and we see it recurring with alarming regularity in certain families. More subtle problems, however, are also passed down through the generations, and the more we are aware of them, the easier we can avoid them.

Please don't misunderstand my point. I am not suggesting that you adopt a fatalistic perspective on fatherhood. We are not in the grip of forces larger than ourselves, fated to behave in certain ways as fathers because of an irresistible genetic impulse. Instead, I am proposing that you can use your free will to escape negative trends and tendencies in your family history if you pay attention to that history. You can achieve this goal no matter what your paternal family history is. You may come from a long line of men who routinely beat their sons for even minor rule infractions, but this doesn't mean that you have to repeat this behavior or even be negatively influenced by it in other ways.

In addition, don't be concerned if you never knew your grandfather or didn't know him well. You'll be able to gather information about him with relative ease either by asking your father directly or by asking some other family member or friend who knew him. I have even worked with men who have discovered information about their grandfathers through letters and journals.

Although you should have gained a good understanding of your feelings toward your father from the exercises in Chapter 2, you need to take the process a step further. You can never fully understand your father, his parenting style, and its impact on you unless you grasp how your grandfather raised him. Every day you interact with your son in ways that can be linked to your grandfather's personality and parenting approach. He was the strong, silent type; your father inherited his reticence; your hatred of your father's long silences has caused you to be overly talkative around your son. Seeing this pattern for what it is will help you to escape its influence.

Of course, you may also discover positive patterns during this investigation, which is terrific. It may be that a strong streak of generosity or mentoring dominates the father-son relationships in your family. While you should be aware of these positive patterns, recognize that negative patterns can coexist with them. People are complex creatures, and as you're beginning to discover, father-son relationships are as complex as they come.

An Example of a Transgenerational Pattern

Transgenerational process is the clinical term describing the legacy that grandfathers, fathers, and sons pass on to the next generation of young men. This process involves behavioral patterns, ideas, and beliefs that flow from generation to generation. While many positive things can be passed from grandfathers to fathers to sons, the negative patterns need to be addressed. Most of you will become aware of this negative inheritance through the indirect method of remembering relationships and asking some questions of third parties to fill in the blanks. To illustrate how powerful this pattern discovery is, however, I would like to share with you the story of Seth, Stan, and Joseph and how Seth's direct discovery will prepare him to be a good father.

Seth has had a tension-filled relationship with his father since adolescence. Seth's father, Stan, frequently criticized Seth for the choices he made. He thought Seth was devoting far too much time to listening to and playing music, telling him that he should devote more time and effort to school. As Seth approached high school graduation, his father was very concerned about Seth's future and pushed him hard to join the military, believing the experience would "shape him up." Seth resisted this pressure until it became so noxious to him that he contacted his grandfather in Oklahoma, who invited him to live with him and go to school there. Seth ended up going to school in Oklahoma and living with his grandfather for two years to save money. Joseph, a retired county employee, struck Seth as being obsessed with two things: professional football and criticizing others. The generous impulse to allow Seth to live with him was the only generosity Seth witnessed in their two years together. Here is how Seth described his grandfather:

> *He was critical and bigoted about everyone and everything. He was verbally abusive to people, and he told me I was an idiot for going to college for music. Grandpa constantly referred to my father as a lazy bum. Grandpa was so negative that I had to move out because I thought I was losing my mind. My father is a saint because he financially supports Grandpa and puts up with his shit. It's amazing that my father even speaks to his dad; I know I wouldn't speak to him if he treated me that way. I understand my father much better now.*

Seth's relationship with his father improved immediately after he lived with his Grandpa Joe and not just because he was relieved to return home. Not only did he gain insight into how his grandfather was as a parent, but he also saw how his grandfather's personality had an impact on how Stan raised him. It was revelatory for Seth, who had never really understood why his father was the way he was. His new perspective allowed him to forgive his father for things he had done in the past, and it allowed Seth and Stan to communicate about their emotional responses to being criticized. By the time Seth turned 24, he and his dad enjoyed a much improved relationship, and the tension between them had diminished. Seth and Stan now have a very close relationship with dramatically less tension between them.

Just as significantly, Seth is now prepared to become a father. He is conscious of the male-pattern criticism in his family. Consciousness of this pattern will both help him to stop himself from following in Joe's and Stan's footsteps and prevent him from overreacting to it and allowing his son to get away with murder.

The Most Common Pattern:
Poor Emotional Communication

Although many negative paternal patterns exist, the most common one involves an inability to communicate thoughts and feelings in a nonjudgmental manner. Joe couldn't communicate with Stan without becoming angry and accusatory; Stan couldn't communicate with Seth without becoming highly critical. When people are unable to express thoughts and feelings—or when they lack the ability to express them honestly to themselves—they often develop relationship and career problems. Marriages end because of a lack of emotional intimacy. People lose friends because they can't speak to them honestly and openly. Professionals receive poor performance reviews because they can't get their points across to their direct reports. One of the great gifts fathers can give their sons is the ability to communicate in the broadest sense of the term. If grandpa is a dysfunctional communicator, though, the odds are that the son and grandson will continue this unfortunate pattern.

Family theorist Murray Bowen suggested that poor family communication evolves generationally. He theorized that if grandfathers, fathers, and sons are left to their own devices, they will become increasingly dysfunctional with each consecutive generation. Dr. Bowen called this concept of family functioning the *multigenerational family (father-son) transmission process*. What's alarming about this theory is that each generation of fathers will become even worse at communicating than the previous generation. This downward spiral needs to be stopped, and the best way to stop is by determining if you, your father, and your grandfather have been operating under the *male gag order*.

In other words, are you part of a multigenerational model in which fathers are "forbidden" to share emotions (with the possible exception of anger) with their sons? I've alluded to this problem earlier—and we'll look at it from other perspectives later—but for now I want you to grasp how this gag order has generational roots. To gain this understanding, determine which of the following traits or responses characterize all three male generations in your family:

____ Never or rarely cries in public

____ Maintains a stoic demeanor in situations where others are highly emotional

____ Refuses to communicate love or sadness to his son through words or gestures

____ Responds to his son's emotional outburst with comments such as "Suck it up" or "Be a man"

____ Never or rarely consoles his son when he is sad or disappointed

____ Has a reputation within the family as the strong, silent type

____ Becomes angry when his son expresses emotion

____ Instructs his son to "develop a thick skin" to deal with life's disappointments

____ Avoids giving or receiving hugs or any physical emotional exchange with his son besides the traditional handshake

____ Refrains from and discourages positive emotional expressions and refuses to celebrate triumphs to show how happy or pleased he is

____ Expresses emotions with great awkwardness and reluctance

____ Says on more than one occasion that men who are emotional are "soft"

If you find that you have made five or more checkmarks, then it's likely that you're in the grip of this pattern and need to make a conscious effort to break it. This means embedding red flags in your mind and waving them like crazy when you catch yourself withholding emotional communication inappropriately. You can tie these red flags to the specific communication sins committed generationally in your family. Maybe none of the three fathers in your family ever talks openly and honestly to his son about how he feels about his work. Or perhaps no one ever is willing to celebrate triumphs joyfully, preferring muted celebrations or none at all. Whatever the paternal pattern is, identify it, watch for it, and make an effort to avoid it. Again, don't expect to break a pattern that has existed for three or more generations in a day, a week, or a month. Your goal initially should be to "manage" the pattern rather than to destroy it.

Becoming Familiar with the Pattern's Negative Impact

Many of my clients find that they become more aware of how this transgenerational pattern affects their own fathering style when they understand how devastating it can be on their sons. It is easy to dismiss the impact if you make false assumptions about it. I've had more than one client say something to the effect of, "Oh, men have always been this way and will always be this way. We just don't do a good job of communicating our emotions, but we turn out okay."

In many families, however, things don't turn out okay. When one generation of fathers is even more emotionally neutered than the next, the son's problems increase exponentially. This is so because at the end of a three-generation cycle, the son is being denied access to love, anger, and sadness. These feelings help a boy to develop his sense of self; they allow him to figure out what he thinks, feels, and desires. When these three emotions are ignored or blocked, they change the course of a boy's life.

Imagine a wedding at which the bride and groom do not express their love to each other. Consider attending a funeral where no one expresses any grief. As strange as this sounds, it probably also reflects the father-son relationships in three generations of your family. The odds are that dads rarely expressed their love or sadness to their sons, and if they expressed anger, its goal was to suppress their sons' emotional expressions. In these situations, sons carry lifetime scars because their fathers never said, "I love you" or "You're important to me" or "I'm proud of you." How different would your life have been if your grandfather had said those things regularly to your father? It is safe to assume that the men in your family would be a lot less angry and aggressive if this type of support, attention, and concern had been passed down from one generation to the next.

Weigh the effect of encouraging sons to suppress emotional expression, especially as this message is passed down through the generations. Your grandfather may have communicated to your father that "men don't cry" in words and through modeling behaviors. Your father may have delivered this message in even stronger terms to you, lecturing about the need to toughen up and reprimanding you when you started to talk about being sad, disappointed, angry, and so on; he even may have forbidden you from hugging him or saying "I love you."

When the feelings of love, sadness, and anger have to be pushed down inside a boy's heart, an emotional fault line begins to develop between him and his father. This boy feels abandoned, neglected, and rejected. He develops a gap in his mind between liking and hating himself, and this gap widens as he grows older. The inability to receive or express feelings makes it very difficult for a boy to have high self-esteem. He naturally assumes that there must be something wrong with him because his father doesn't tell him he loves him. When he can't release the emotions bubbling up inside of him, the emotional pressure builds within, and at some point in the future it's likely to explode— he may take out his rage on a spouse or, even more likely, on his son.

If this pattern exists in two or more generations of your family, you need to take action now so that you don't end up doing even more damage to your son than your father did to you.

Reversing the Transgenerational Trend

Allen, a 68-year-old retired University of California professor of speech communication, told me

Growing up in Texas in the 1930s and 1940s was tough; my father would have died if I told him I wanted to express my feelings. There was no such thing as feeling overwhelmed or sad; you just kept it all inside with a stiff upper lip. I think this repression was so much for me that I unconsciously pursued a speech communication career. I would have died as an adult if I didn't learn to communicate my thoughts and feelings. My father was a banker and very religious. He loved to drink whiskey on Saturday night. When he drank he was a lot nicer to me. He was only emotional after a half bottle of Jack Daniels. My father would tell me he loved me when he was drunk but never sober.

In Allen's family, men were only allowed to be lovingly emotional when drunk. Anger was an acceptable emotion, but it often was expressed as hostility rather than in a caring manner. It is not surprising, therefore, that part of Allen's inheritance was a drinking problem. Until his thirties, Allen's life was a mess. His wife and son left him because of his drinking and his emotional miserliness, and it was only after their departure that he went into his cave and began exploring his father's and grandfather's lack of emotional expression. Or rather, he grasped that when they were sober, they kept their feelings hidden and expected their sons to follow suit.

Fortunately, Allen was able to see the pattern that had dominated the fathers in his family and rise above it. Although it took him a number of years, he learned how to share feelings of love, sadness, and anger with others when he was sober. His son, Alex, is the beneficiary of this change. After the divorce, Allen reconnected with his son and was able not only to talk about and show his feelings in front of him but also explain the fathering pattern in their family. Part of their discussion involved how men in the family had become alcoholics, and this fact encouraged Alex to vow never to drink. More significantly, Allen explained how his father had modeled the type of stoic, "he man" behavior that was antithetical to living a full, meaningful life. He endorsed womanizing and drinking but kept their father-son communication focused on activities—sports, local politics, and jobs. Allen added that his father's father had been a similar type of parent and that everyone said that his dad was a "chip off the old block."

Alex became the first male in the family for three generations not to have a problem with liquor. Even more important, Alex was a loving, empathetic father to his three boys. He made a conscious effort to tell them he loved them every night before they went to bed, and he didn't try to hide his sadness when something bad happened. Alex broke the pattern in part because Allen changed his fathering behaviors after the divorce and after he had emerged from his cave. It also was critical, however, that Allen shared the emotional dysfunction story with his son. By fostering awareness of the generational problems the men in the family were heir to, he gave Alex the information he needed to avoid falling into the same trap.

Identifying the Fathering Flaws— and Passing on Only the Information

A little knowledge goes a long way toward breaking the fathering pattern in your family. Ideally, you will pass on the knowledge to your son of the fathering flaws handed down from one generation to the next, and this knowledge will enable your son to avoid slipping into the same behavioral patterns. It also will help him to better understand you, just as it will help you to better understand your father. This understanding can dissipate the resentment, bitterness, and anger that lingers long after a father is gone.

Earlier I asked you to place checkmarks next to traits and responses indicative of fathering problems through the generations in your family. That exercise will help to prepare you for the following one, which asks you to be more specific about the negative traits that have been handed down from fathers to sons in your family.

1. List five negative behavioral traits of yourself, your father, and your grandfather. These can be anything from a quick temper to poor listening skills to impulsiveness. They also may involve issues of absence, neglect, or abuse. For instance: "He was never around." The goal is to define who each person is from a negative standpoint. Don't worry about trying to find similar traits for all three of you; that will come in the fourth step.

Grandfather	Father	You

2. Examine the traits listed and create a parallel list of the negative effect each trait had on other people. For instance, you may have listed "insulting" under your grandfather. The effect of this trait, then, might be "makes others feel stupid." To some extent, you will have to speculate about some of these effects, although you should feel free to do a bit of research about your grandfather if necessary so that you feel more comfortable with the effect listed.

Grandfather	Father	You

3. Now be more specific and delineate the effect in relationship to each son. For instance, the effect of "makes others feel stupid" might be translated to "makes him (my father) very reticent around his father." In some instances, you may find that the general effect on others is essentially the same as the specific one related to father and son.

Grandfather	Father	You

4. Examine the preceding list for similar effects. Are all the sons relatively quiet around their fathers? It doesn't have to be an exact parallel. For instance, your grandfather could have made your father reluctant to speak when he was around, and your father could have made you choose your words carefully before you spoke to him. Write the similar effects below.

5. How do these effects translate into emotional terms? In other words, if the key effect was a reluctance to speak one's mind in father's presence, then a possible emotional translation might be, "We weren't encouraged to share how we felt." Or you might be able to be more specific: "No father wanted to hear his son express his fears." Fill in the key emotional effect below.

I recognize that this exercise isn't simple, and you may draw a blank when it comes to some of the steps. To facilitate the process, request help from other family members who know you, your father, or your grandfather. It is also acceptable to leave some blanks. You will still draw a good picture of the fathering pattern even if you have some question marks or have to make some guesses.

When your son is old enough to have a conversation about this subject—at least 10 years old—start introducing this information to him. Let him know that you feel badly that your father and his father before him were gone so much that you never had the opportunity to share your feelings with them, and that you are not going to make the same mistake. You don't have to make a big deal out of this conversation, especially if your child is still relatively young. What you do want, though, is to introduce the knowledge into his life and return to it occasionally. In this way you remind both him and yourself of your transgenerational Achilles heel. This awareness will help you to break the pattern.

Thought-Provoking Questions

Although these exercises may not be as emotionally painful as those in Chapter 2, they do touch some raw nerves. It is scary to see a pattern emerge that has you in its grip. Once you identify it, though, you need to ask yourself some questions. Don't stop the investigation process when you figure out that you come from a family of emotionally cold fathers or whatever you discover. Explore the nuances and ramifications of this pattern. If you want, talk about it with a trusted advisor or with a loved one. Again, the goal is awareness. You are going to be a much better father to your son if you possess an intimate grasp of the fathering breakdowns in your family tree.

I've created a list of questions that supplement the previous five-step exercise. These questions represent a less formal approach that might be better suited to your personality or that help you do the five-step exercise with more accuracy and insight. They are also a good way to bring out the positive patterns that I emphasized earlier.

As you go through these questions, please be honest with yourself and as spontaneous as you can be. As they say about taking tests in school, the first answer is usually the right one. Let the truth emerge, and then roll the answer around in your mind.

- How did your grandfather express love to your father? Did your father feel loved by his father?
- How would your father describe his relationship with his father? What would your grandfather say about your father as a son growing up?
- What would your father say about you growing up?
- What did your father tell you about love, and how did he express it to you? Do you feel loved by your father, and did you feel that way when you were younger? Does your son consider himself loved by you?
- How important is your father's approval to you? Do you feel that at this point in your life you have this approval? How important was your grandfather's approval to your father?
- What were your grandfather's expectations of your father growing up? How did those multigenerational expectations affect how you were raised?
- Do you feel comfortable with strong emotional feelings and the expression of them? How have the men in your family dealt with talking about emotional issues?
- How have your grandfather, father, and you dealt with loss?
- What is the primary emotion that your father has expressed to you? What emotion did your grandfather show your father?
- How did or do your grandfather and father deal with the issue of death?
- What was the biggest loss in your grandfather's life and your father's life? Did they or do they ever talk about it?
- What has been the biggest loss in your life? Does your father know about it? And if so, what was his response to it?
- What role have rejection, abandonment, and neglect played in your father's life? What symbolic wounds to your father's head and heart did he experience from your grandfather? Have you and your father ever talked about these wounds?
- How has anger been used to cover up the emotional wounds in your life? How have your father and grandfather used anger?

- What is the main piece of advice your father gave you growing up? Do you believe it and use it?
- What pattern of behavior, thinking, or being would you like to continue from your grandfather and father? Name at least one positive pattern.
- If you father or grandfather has passed away, do you miss him? What do you miss about him and why?
- What is the greatest impact that your grandfather had on your father? What is the impact that he had or has on your life? Consider short-term and lasting behavioral patterns.
- How would your grandmother describe your grandfather's relationship with your father? How would your son's mother describe your father and son relationship?
- What issues in your opinion are unresolved between your grandfather and father?
- What issues seem unresolved between you and your father? What can you do to resolve them?
- What role did physical violence have in your relationship with your father? How physically violent was your grandfather and father's relationship?
- How important is your father to your son? What role would you like your father to have with your son?
- What is one thing that your father is very proud of you for?
- What is one thing you would like your son to learn from your relationship with your father?

Making Good Use of Your Answers

As you reflect on the answers to these questions, you may find disturbing "themes" that run through the paternal side of your family. Some men are profoundly upset to discover that they have unknowingly perpetuated a harmful legacy. They often feel guilty that they are the third in a line of flawed fathers.

If you feel upset and guilty, though, this is a good sign. Use these feelings to break the pattern. Recognize that you have put yourself in a position to be a good father to your son precisely because you have identified this pattern. Perhaps anger is the only acceptable emotion that men in your family display toward their sons. Perhaps you, your father, and your grandfather all have an aversion to expressions of sadness and disappointment. Maybe you come from a line of strong, silent types.

Whatever the pattern is, start working to change the fathering style you've inherited. A good preliminary exercise to foster this change involves creating two simple lists based on your answers to the preceding list of questions. First, create a list of qualities that the men in your family possess that you absolutely do not want your son to inherit. Second, create a list of male family qualities that you hope your son will acquire. As you'll discover, these two lists will serve as loose parameters for adapting your parenting style to meet the needs of your son.

4

Fathering with Style

My father was always very critical of me and the things I did. He never let up on me, never. I do not want to be that way with my son. I want to raise him in a more supportive atmosphere and not be so distant and critical of him. I will be different from my father—it will be my style, not his.

David, age 41

I have no role models or example that I want to follow for fathering. My father was gone out of my life from the point of conception and has never been involved. I am doing this father thing by the seat of my pants. My main goal is to be a good father to my son.

Robert, age 37

A T THIS POINT YOU recognize your power and responsibility as a father, you are aware of how your own father influenced the way you treat your son, and you have identified the three-generation pattern of which you are a part. This preliminary work has prepared you for the process of identifying and improving your parenting style. You are now much more conscious of how profoundly your attitudes, actions, and words affect your son's development and the quality of your relationship. You also know that a historical context influences the way you father— that knowledge of how your father and grandfather operated will provide you with valuable insights about how to be—and how not to be—a father.

You have a certain way of interacting with your son that is part of who you are as an individual and who you are as a son and a grandson.

Your personality joins with your childhood/adolescent experiences to shape your parenting style. While you unconsciously incorporate traits of your father and grandfather into how you parent, you consciously try to choose an alternative path. In a 1995 study, over 3000 men were asked if they wanted to father (raise) their son the way they were fathered. An astounding 93 percent of the men answered, "No."

Given this desire to be a different type of father and yet the tendency to slip into old fathering patterns, you need to define and refine your style to best serve your son.

The Five Styles

Five fundamental styles of fathering exist, and each has its own pattern, rhythm, and emotional, mental, and physical methods. While you may employ elements of all five styles, one of them predominates. The styles are

- Superachiever
- Time bomb
- Passive
- Absent
- Compassionate/mentor

Before discussing each of these styles, let's examine what a fathering style is all about. Every parent–child relationship has distinct and tangible characteristics. The way your father communicated to you had a definite pattern. The primary times when he would communicate may have been confined to specific situations and modes: under stress, when angry, through screaming, or when you were in huge trouble. Your father also may have communicated with you only when things were fine, and your mother intervened when there were problems. Even if your father was often or always absent, this constitutes a style, at least in the sense that it had an impact on you as a child and colors the style you use with your son.

When I talk about fathering style, I am not referring to superficial or interest-based characteristics. Certainly some fathers emphasize sports with their sons, and other dads focus on education and good grades. These interests are just small elements of a larger style. Think about all the opportunities and situations in which fathers and sons interact:

meals, playing catch, bedtime stories, serious father-son discussions on specific topics, in the presence of others, and so on. Each interaction has a different setting and goal, but the father's style is overarching. It manifests itself in the way he says goodnight and in the way he asks questions about school.

Finally, this style is eminently mutable. As you can see from the list of five styles, one is clearly the ideal. Most of you, however, probably have touches of this ideal, but one of the other four is dominant. This makes perfect sense because if you possessed the ideal style, you probably wouldn't be compelled to pick up this book in the first place. The good news is that all fathers are capable of making the ideal style their own.

Let's now define each style.

Superachiever

This is the father who can do it all and then some. He is extremely capable with whatever task, project, or challenge he takes on. His work ethic is clear to everyone who knows him: Win. This father measures his own and his sons' self-worth solely by accomplishment. For example, Tim, age 34 and engaged, came to see me because he was extremely critical toward his fiancée and his employees. By way of explanation for his behavior, Tim said, "Nothing I ever did was good enough for my dad. Straight A's were just expected. I never felt good enough for him. My employees feel like they cannot try hard enough and I am always critical of them." Tim, like so many men whose fathers exhibit the superachiever style, suffered silently, hoping to win his father's approval. The desire to gain this approval is built into our DNA and is a process that all sons go through. All sons at all ages want their fathers' unspoken and spoken approbation. Boys learn at a young age to thrive on their fathers' approval, or they learn that it is not coming their way. Boys who don't receive their fathers' support develop a sense of loss in their life at an early age.

The fundamental breakdown between the superachiever father and son results in the "not good enough" syndrome. In the Pat Conroy novel, *Great Santini,* the story is about a father who will not and cannot accept that his son is going to surpass him physically, mentally, and emotionally. The ongoing power struggle between father and son eventually results in the son's spirit being broken. As a result, this father is forever locked into a place of insecurity about his own self-worth. Neither man receives the approval and love each craves from the other. Both walk away from the relationship wounded and bitter. If Conroy were ever to write a sequel, it would be about how this son became a man who had constant battles with other authority figures.

The superachiever father is a man who never received nurturing from his father. In order to compensate for this loss of emotional support, he develops a competitive nature that is always looking for perfection in work, relationships, or anything else that will cover up the loss of relationship with his father. Part and parcel of this competitiveness is a hypercritical nature. This is one reason men frequently engage in cruel teasing; such teasing is a way of unloading all the anger and self-hatred they harbor. It is also the reason they constantly criticize and are hostile to their sons. As fathers get in their verbal digs, spend little time with their sons, and always ask for perfects, these sons feel like losers if they are not the best at whatever they are doing. Eventually these boys reach a breaking point with their fathers. Many times the defining episode will result in a physical altercation that is damaging to both men. Physical violence is very common in this style of fathering. It is a way of keeping the son on the straight and narrow and for the father to feel like the king of the house.

Some boys react to this type of father by becoming passive, compliant, depressed, and underachieving. Others, however, act out. In my work as a Los Angeles police officer for 8 years and my subsequent psychological research on teenage boys who act out, I have seen boys respond to superachiever fathers with great rage. They become a danger to both themselves and others.

The passive son will rebel against his father by not doing his homework, failing in school, dropping out, and getting married at a young age. He will have great difficulty focusing on a career, education, relationships, and himself. There is a chronic sense of "stuckness" that prevails in all his choices. This son will find himself at age 40 still wondering what he is going to do with his life. The underlying problem: He does not want to be a high achiever like his father. This fear of becoming like his father causes him to run from any type of adultlike commitment or challenge. Functioning well below his capabilities, this boy will learn how to self-medicate with drugs to keep a safe emotional distance from his true feelings and aspirations. As you might guess, this son exacts revenge on his father by being indifferent to the type of success that is so important to the superachiever.

The sons who act out gravitate toward risk and danger, and they often end up in trouble with the police. Underneath the tough-guy exterior, though, are little boys who are angry about their fathers' lack of attention. The breach between these men is difficult to mend. Regardless of mothers' interventions to heal the relationship, the tension remains high. Many times moms are forced to pick sides, and again, the sons feel betrayed. Another split between these fathers and sons occurs when the boys get in trouble with the law, and the father responds by saying something to the effect of, "I disown you."

Here's an example of a superachiever father and the acting-out son. At 42, Hal appears to be a "cool surfer dude." He is trim, fit, and suntanned. Then, on closer inspection, Hal reveals a stressed look that makes others uncomfortable. Hal came to me to discuss his failed marriage, dead-end job, marijuana addiction, and desire to run from his problems. At our first meeting, Hal made the following statement with a scary lack of emotion:

I have done it all. I have worked as a carpenter, movie director, cook, and currently I am a computer programmer for a bank. I have had 10 different jobs in the last 15 years. I have not put much of myself into anything since the fifth grade. I got straight A's in the fifth grade. My father laughed and said no big deal; he did that all through school. I said to myself at age 11, screw it; I am out of here and checked out. School after that was just serving time; it pissed my father off to no end. In high school I found two great drugs: surfing and marijuana. I have been coasting ever since elementary school. My father was so tough on me growing up because he knew I was smarter than him, and he couldn't accept that. He is now 79 years old; a millionaire a hundred times over, and still is after my ass. My ex-wife thinks I am a flake, but it's not that. I just don't want to become like him. It scares the shit out of me, and it is why I don't want children.

Hal began to come to therapy to discuss his marijuana addiction and how he has avoided adult responsibility based on his father's chronic criticisms. Hal knew that if he was ever going to have children, which he actually wanted despite his fear of being a father, he had to confront the father in his head and stop avoiding those painful feelings and thoughts. Hal became aware that he could become the father he always wanted by truly embracing his past relationship with his father and move forward as an adult man, not as a rebellious, underachieving son who is only damaging his own life.

Time Bomb

This style of fathering is based solely on the fear factor. Authority in this house is maintained by sheer volume of emotional expression. The use of threatening language, anger, yelling, and promises of physical violence are the status quo. The norm is the unpredictability of this father's response to anything and everything. A harmless comment such as "How was your day, Dad?" can set off an explosion. These explosions do not have to be alcohol-related but many times are fueled by it. The son of this father is also in a constant state of chaos and fear. He looks terrified and fearful much of the time, and nothing feels safe for this boy.

This boy is the first stop for the father's abuse in all its forms—physical, emotional, verbal, sexual, and mental. It is not necessarily what the father says that is disturbing but the way it is wrapped up in a ball of fire and hatred. Everyone in the house is sensitized to this phenomenon. In order to survive, the son learns to develop amazing people-pleasing skills early on.

Sons of time bomb fathers carry vivid painful experiences and feelings. These sons are truly survivors. A close friend of mine, Roy, is one of these surviving sons. Roy over the years has told me bits and pieces about his childhood and his fear of repeating it with his 11-year-old son. When we attended a football game with our sons, he said:

Steve, you have no idea of what happened between me and my father. He would physically beat me every night for no reason at all. He punched me out at least once a month as a teenager. I had a lot of problems growing up; it was my father and his insane behavior. No one in the neighborhood messed with my father. My mother just tried to keep the peace the best she could. My sister, Nancy, just hates him now. He never beat her, just me. Then, after he beat me, he would verbally beat the shit out of me and was always on my ass about my appearance.

Interestingly, time bomb fathers can be very successful at work and save their explosiveness for their families or even just their sons. This is so because this man feels particularly vulnerable in his role as a father, and he covers up this vulnerability with rage. It is almost as if when he looks at his son he sees his own vulnerability reflected back, and this enrages him.

I had the opportunity to speak with Norm, the time bomb father of my friend Roy. Norm is now 75 years old. He was very pleasant in answering my questions; he didn't seem at all defensive or angry. In fact, Norm admitted that he wasn't the greatest father in the world. He said:

> *I didn't do a very good job in raising him; his mother did. I was just crazy at times in how I handled him and myself. I would do it very differently today; I lost control too many times. Things were tough on me—no education, I was always hustling. I didn't mean to take out my anger on Roy the way I did; it was just a bad habit. He turned out just fine even though I was hard on him. He went to college and has a beautiful son. I am proud of him.*

I asked Norm what else would he do differently today if he were raising a son. Norm looked me straight in the eye and said:

> *I would spend more time with my son. I was gone too much, chasing a buck. I spent too much time away from home, and I now regret it. I am always telling Roy not to follow my example because it is not a good one. He can do better at fathering than I did. I got crazy way too much, and now my son and daughter are both reluctant to be close to me. They are scared of me. It's a shame, but Roy tries hard in spite of our past. I am glad we talk as much as we do [once a week].*

What I find hopeful about this story is that Roy transcended the time bomb style of parenting. Despite the physical abuse, Roy is not a time bomb father himself. By going into the cave and dealing with all the negative emotions of his childhood, he has become the type of involved, empathic father we all aspire to be. After describing the remaining three styles, I will focus on how you can overcome whatever negative style you were raised with or that you now exhibit.

Passive

Mainstream culture refers to this father as the "1950s Ozzie Nelson, 'Leave It to Beaver,' 'Father Knows Best' " type. He is stable, consistent, hard working, calm, and reserved. He would never contemplate or engage in any type of destructive behavior toward his son, family, or self. A client once told me that the running family joke was, "Is dad dead or just sleeping on the couch?" His father was always on the outside of family life, just sort of watching from a distance.

What is missing for this father and son is a strong emotional connection. While they don't fight or have any animosity between them, they also lack energy, understanding, or willingness to display love toward and support for one another. This mainstream father does not embrace his son but rather embraces the routine. The mother is this family's emotional center.

On the surface, this fathering style may seem ideal. After all, this dad is comfortable allowing his son to express his ideas, even if they are different from his or society's norms. A passive father feels that it is his duty to support his son despite a difference of opinion. This passive approach, though, has a hidden downside. Sons of passive fathers grow into men who, in their thirties and forties, find themselves unable to express themselves emotionally. Since mom handled the emotional expression duties in the families, the son assumes that his wife also will take on this role. In today's environment, however, Ozzie will not make Harriet happy; she expects him to be more emotionally involved in Ricky's and David's lives.

Fathers in the 1950s showed their love through actions rather than words. The crisis for sons of passive fathers involves incorporating the values of their fathers into their own roles as parents and learning to translate these values into emotional language. The challenge of a contemporary marriage—the division of household duties, more child-raising responsibilities, the need for greater emotional intimacy—causes them to panic. They aren't prepared to become the father they want to be; they stammer and stutter when it comes to articulating feelings to their sons. It is tremendously frustrating for these fathers because they know the right way to relate to their sons, but they lack the training and skills to implement this fathering approach.

To understand the ramifications of being a passive father, let's look at the relationships between grandfather Pat (age 80), father Mark (age 53), and grandson Paul (age 18). Pat, a classic passive type, has led an admirable life. He's been happily married to the same woman for 54 years, had an excellent, fulfilling job in the aerospace industry, and has good relationships with Mark and his other children. In fact, Mark can't remember a time when his father complained about any issue in his life or became seriously angry at anyone in the family. Growing up, Mark was convinced that his father had everything figured out, and more than one of Mark's friends told him how lucky he was to have Pat as a father.

Mark's life has been more difficult than his father's. A banker, he was fired recently from a job he liked, and he's been struggling to deal with this rejection. On top of that, he was divorced a few years ago from Paul's mother. Although he has remarried, he is still struggling with all the postdivorce issues, such as visitation and "competing" for Paul's affection with Paul's new stepfather. In counseling, Mark told me that he feels like a failure. He frequently compares his life with that of his father and feels that he comes up short. He often feels overwhelmed and confused about how to deal with Paul's adolescent anger. Mark has tried to talk with his father about these problems, but Pat does what he has always done when Mark has attempted a heart-to-heart conversation: He rubs his forehead like he has a headache and tells him not to worry, everything will work out. Once, when Mark was 10 or so, he remembers being bitterly disappointed when he failed to make his Little League team. He came home in tears and rushed toward his father. Rather than comfort him or allow him to express his disappointment or even yell at him for being a crybaby, Pat ignored the tears and started talking about a completely different subject.

Through his therapy, Mark recognizes that his father's passive style has made it difficult for him to deal with emotion, especially when it comes to his son. Nonetheless, he has been making a concerted effort to deal with Paul on emotional rather than purely intellectual terms. It is difficult for him because he often feels tongue-tied when he has to address a sensitive topic, such as Paul's angry outbursts when Mark insists that he adhere to certain rules. Still, Mark is making progress, in large part because he is aware of his father's parenting style and how it affected him.

Absent

As we've discussed, this absent style can be figurative or literal. In its subtlest form, the absentee dad is similar to the passive one in that he's not emotionally engaged with his son. Unlike a passive father, however, the absentee type opts out of family life. He isn't merely emotionally disengaged, but he seems unwilling to make an effort to participate in family activities or even talk much with his son. Given a choice between watching his son play ball or working late, he'll choose the latter almost every time. The passive father at least is a presence in the family; the absent one isn't.

The literally absent father takes it a step further by physically abandoning his son. We can all understand a difficult relationship with a partner, but the complete rejection of a son is mind-boggling. This fathering style goes beyond divorce because a significant percentage of postdivorce fathers actually become more involved with their sons. The father instigates an emotional, mental, and physical break that the son perceives as rejection, no matter what age he is when it occurs.

The worst example of an absent father is the deadbeat dad. Men who abandon their children physically and financially don't just do psychological harm, but they can deny their son educational, cultural, and other opportunities that are important to his development and future success. Still, providing financial support without emotional support is tremendously harmful to boys. It is also harmful to be physically present but emotionally or intellectually absent. These father have no clue about what is going on in their sons' lives. This type of absent style sends a negative message to the son about his importance to his father.

All types of absent fathering lead to the son's profound sadness and anger. The natural psychological response to a loss is fear, pain, and then anger to cover up the wound. Sons who experience the loss of fathers all go through this process. A father's death is also a loss, but his involuntary departure versus a voluntary exit creates a different type of effect on the son.

Absent fathers create a "paradox of feelings" in their boys. Sons naturally wonder if the untrustworthy qualities that mark an absent father are also present in them. They have seen their mothers' resentment and anger toward him because he has left them alone to raise their sons. Many times the abandoned wife's resentment and anger extend beyond the father to all men. This confuses boys because they are males whom their mothers love, yet they also are going to be men whom their mothers hate.

Typically, boys cope with absent fathers in a number of ways. First, they become overachievers, attempting to be the man their fathers never were and thereby please their mothers. Second, they personalize their fathers' indifference and rejection, assuming that they are at fault for his departure. Third, they take their anger out on society and people closest to them.

Trusting relationships are difficult for sons of absent fathers to form. This is why so many of them have difficulty working for others, especially male bosses. These sons often gravitate toward self-employment because they don't want to take a chance of interacting with another male authority figure who could wound them as their fathers did. These men often aren't sure why they distrust, disdain, and dislike male authority figures, and this lack of insight may seem irrational to an outside perspective.

At 25, Seth has struggled with his knowledge that he had an absent father. When he was a high school senior, he had a drinking problem and no life direction. His parents had divorced when he was 10 years old, and he hadn't seen his father since that time. When he was 17, I asked him what he thought about his family situation. Seth said:

> *I understand why my parents got divorced. I was only 10, but I knew my mom and dad were not happy. My dad was always verbally abusive, and now he acts like he is the victim. He moved to the Midwest after the divorce and has never come back to California to see my sister or me. He has never invited us out to his house and never calls or writes. I don't call either, but what am I going to say? Be my father? He dropped us like a hot potato. I sort of hate him because he forgot me. I don't know how you blow off your kids.*

Seth and I met on and off for the next 5 years until he went away to college at age 23. He struggled with finding a focus and liking himself enough to stop abusing alcohol. Seth made a commitment to himself to attend school and reconnect with his father in the Midwest. Six years after our initial meeting, Seth told me:

> *I needed to find my father and face the fear of being rejected again. I was blaming myself, but now I know that his leaving me had nothing to do with me. It is his issue, but I had to settle that with myself. I am going to*

be okay at school. I am a music major, something my father always laughed at, but I love music, and I feel that is my gift. I accept that my father isn't what I want in a father. The pain in my heart did stop once I acknowledged my longing for a father. Now I have a plan and some understanding that I didn't cause him to leave us. I feel much better that he really left for other reasons.

Compassionate/Mentor

The compassionate/mentor (C/M) style, as the name implies, combines emotional intelligence with a wise teacher approach. Sons feel that their dads are making them their number one priority, and fathers are willing to do whatever it takes to raise their sons properly. This style of fathering involves providing an emotional safe harbor in which the toddler, preteen, and young man feels that he can take chances, fail, and still be surrounded by his father's love.

As part of the C/M style, fathers help their sons learn how to reason. This may seem like a relatively innocuous task, but fathers who help their sons reason allow for the differences of opinions that independent reasoning produces. Rather than ignore or mock their sons' arguments, these fathers encourage their boys to think for themselves. By respecting their sons' ideas and thought processes, these fathers help them to develop respect and understanding for other people's ideas, including those of their own sons.

C/M fathers also provide emotional support to their sons. Because these boys have felt their fathers' love, they are able to love and support others. They spend time together in myriad activities—eating, athletics, doing homework, playing on the floor, and participating in numerous other endeavors. As a result, a bond exists between them that allows them to communicate with each other during even difficult times.

I should emphasize, however, that the C/M style does not mean perfection. These fathers make mistakes, as do their sons. They may lose their tempers at these boys when they are making noise or engage in arguments with their adolescent sons about curfew and other typical topics. At the same time, though, these fathers and sons enjoy the type of bond that can survive whatever disagreements or mistakes they make. These fathers don't pretend to be perfect, and they are willing to admit that they are wrong, at least in some situations. They do, however, teach their sons to be forgiving by being forgiving of their sons' errors.

Dave and Pete illustrate this particular fathering style. Dave, age 48, is a developer, and his father, Pete, age 80, is a retired house painter and carpenter. Pete has lived with Dave and his family for the last 5 years. Dave is married and has two boys, and he is an only child as a result of his baby brother dying of sudden infant death syndrome (SIDS) 45 years ago. That death changed the course of Pete's and Dave's relationship. After the death, Dave's mother never hugged or kissed him again. Dave was only 3 years old at the time. Recognizing his wife's emotional withdrawal from their son, Pete made a commitment to himself that he would be a compassionate father to his son. He hugged his son every day and was especially sensitive to his emotional needs. Remarkably, Pete developed this fathering style in the 1950s and 1960s, when most fathers avoided nurturing their sons.

I asked Pete how did he know to be so compassionate with his son. Pete said:

> *I knew that my son needed me to be more than just a bread winner . . . [to be] a strong father. I could feel his pain, and his mother couldn't get past the death of our second child. I knew that if I didn't help Dave and love him, no one was going to. I was his Little League coach and Boy Scout leader, and now I advise him on the custom homes he builds. I knew I needed to stay close to Dave and that has never changed. Now I get to play with my grandsons, and that is something wonderful.*

I asked Dave about his father and what he thinks of their relationship. Dave said:

> *I don't know where I would be if it wasn't for my dad and his support. He has always been my rock and backboard. We didn't have much money growing up, and I always thought that's okay, I have my dad. Now my sons get to watch my dad and me get along, and it is good for all of us. My father is one in a million; he has never dropped the ball or let me down. He has always found a way to work and keep all of us going. Now he is my right hand man with the business. He is the voice of reason for me, and I am very lucky to have such a father. I don't know what I would do without him.*

Again, it's not that Pete is a perfect father; they both admit to disagreements. At the same time, their relationship lacks the tension, anger, and unresolved issues that mark many father-son relationships. Pete's compassion and mentoring role not only has created a strong bond between them, but also it has helped Dave become a similarly terrific father to his own sons.

Making Adjustments: How to Add Compassion and Mentoring to Your Style

As you read the description of each style, you probably immediately recognized your own dominant approach or the manner in which your father raised you. It may be that you and your father—and your grandfather, for that matter—all have different styles. Your dad may have been the time bomb type, for instance, but his rages turned you into a passive type—you found he was less likely to explode if you were quiescent. You carried that passive approach into your own parenting and bent over backwards to avoid raising your voice to your son, and in the process, you sacrificed any real emotional connection with him. Although you may have discovered certain pattern similarities between you, your father, and your grandfather, you also may find that your styles are different.

The key is recognizing your own style and making adjustments in the direction of compassion and mentoring. To help you make these adjustments, I have provided some tips and techniques under each of the four styles. Don't expect them to produce changes overnight. Again, the key is awareness and a willingness to change for the sake of your son. As you will discover, though, even small dollops of compassion and mentoring can have an extraordinarily positive influence on your father-son relationship and your son's attitudes and actions.

Superachiever

- *Keep a "criticism" journal* for a week in which you enter any remarks you make that are directly critical of your son. It can include entries as simple as, "You need to do better than that in math" to a more detailed description of your criticisms. At the end of the week, total the number of critical comments. The following week, be conscious of your criticisms, and try to reduce this number by at least one. Keep a journal for this second week to see if you can achieve this goal. If you do, try to reduce the number by at least one for the third week. Keep at it until you reduce the criticisms by 50 percent from the original total.

- *Practice complimenting* your son. By practicing, I mean thinking about specific things your son says or does that merit your approval and support. If he is a young child, you might compliment him on his ability to build blocks. If he is a teenager, it might be a subject that he does well at, whether it's in school or an outside interest. The rehearsal will help you to overcome your natural inclination to criticize. Concentrate on what it is that he cares about, that he tries hard to do well at, or that he shows promise at when engaged in an activity. Resolve to tell him that he did a good job or that you appreciate his hard work. It doesn't have to be an eloquent speech, and you shouldn't tell him he's good at something that he clearly isn't good at. You also shouldn't lay it on too thick or shower him with compliments. You'll find that a little sugar goes a long way, so practice what you want to say to him, and then say it.

Time Bomb

Videotape yourself exploding when no one else is around. Set up a videotape camera and record yourself reproducing a recent tirade against your son. Make sure that he is not around, and then attempt to come as close as possible to what you said and did when you exploded on your child. Don't hold back. Try to mirror the words, tone of voice, and physical gestures or expressions that you used. Once you're done, watch the video and put yourself in your son's place. Imagine being on the receiving end of your tirade. Think about what he must be feeling as he's listening to your angry words and seeing your reddened face. Ask yourself if this is the main memory of you that you want him to carry into adulthood.

Create a substitute action for your physical or verbal assaults on
your son. In other words, think of an alternative way to
vent your anger when you feel it starting to boil over. It may
be something as simple as getting into your car or some other
isolated environment and letting loose a scream. It may involve
going outside and shooting baskets or running around the block.
By having this alternative action firmly planted in your mind,
you've given yourself an escape route from the spanking or
shaking that is your reflex to anger at your son.

Passive

- Test your *emotional exchange capacity.* Review the following list of
  common ways fathers create emotional bonds with their sons, and
  place a checkmark next to the ones that you regularly employ:
  ___ Hugging him
  ___ Allowing him to see you cry
  ___ Laughing together
  ___ Communicating to him through words and gestures when
     you are disappointed about something that happened to you
  ___ Venting healthy anger—anger without hostility—against
     everyone from your boss to a disappointing sports team in
     his presence
  ___ Telling him how you feel when someone close to you dies
  ___ Allowing him to accompany you to funerals, weddings,
     family reunions, and other emotionally charged events
  ___ Encouraging him to tell you how he feels and not judging
     his emotion or trying to tell him he shouldn't feel this way
- Use this list as a guide for establishing an emotional connection
  with your son, trying to engage in at least a few of these activities
  with him weekly.
- *Start with small emotional expressions* when interacting with
  your son, and build on them. For instance, you may find it
  uncomfortable to hug your son initially. Therefore, start by
  patting him on the back or even shaking his hand. These small
  physical connections will provide both you and your son with

positive feedback and will allow each of you to warm up to each other. It also might be difficult for you to tell him you love him at first. Try to be more specific with what you love about him. For instance, "I love the way you hit the ball" or "I really enjoy the way you sing, 'Old MacDonald Had a Farm.' "

Absent

Increase the *amount of time* you spend with you son in increments. In a worst-case scenario, if you haven't seen your son in weeks or months, start with as little as an hour weekly. If you've simply been spending long hours in the office, try coming home an hour early one day a week when you know your son will be home. Increase the time you're together slowly so that it feels like a natural progression both to you and to him.

Increase the *quality time* you spend with your son. Although quality time has become a bit of a cliché, it is a valid concept, especially for fathers who often put in token appearances. Try to get your son involved in something that interests you; your natural enthusiasm for the endeavor will be felt by your son, and he will want to please you by trying to like the activity, especially if he's not yet an adolescent. At the same time, figure out what interests him, and make an effort to be a participant in that interest. This can be difficult for some fathers, especially if they have adolescent sons whose primary interest is heavy metal music that they find irritating. Nonetheless, it doesn't take much effort for you to look up a heavy metal group on the Web, listen to their music, and talk to your son about why he likes them. This often leads to a real, meaningful exchange between father and son rather than the customary empty inquiries such as "How was school today?" or "What did you do last night?"

No matter which of these four fathering styles you employ, these activities will move you a little closer to the compassionate/mentoring style. Don't expect to make an immediate and complete transition to this style just by doing these activities. A major obstacle most men face is feeling like a "lost son," a feeling that keeps them mired in their current style. Let's look at how you can jettison this lost son perspective.

5

— ❧ ❧ —

Growing Up

How to Leave the Lost Boy Behind

Can't a father make up for 30 years of screw-ups? All I wanted to do was make everything all right. I wanted to make up for being a lousy father.
Gene Hackman's character, speaking to his youngest son in the
movie *The Royal Tannenbaums*

It took me a long time to finally accept that I never had much of a connection to my father—that my dad invested very little in our relationship. I have faced the empty feelings I have always had, not having a father's support, and now—with two young sons of my own—I am learning how to be a good father to myself so that I can be a better father to them.
William, age 46

To become a more compassionate, mentoring father, you need to come to terms with being a lost son. By lost, I'm referring to feelings of loss and abandonment that most boys experience, even if their fathers seemed like model dads. Make no mistake about it: Whether your father was neglectful, verbally or physically abusive, emotionally unavailable, or physically absent, you are a lost son. Coping with these issues, feelings, and life experiences is critical to becoming the father you want to be. No matter what your current fathering style is, you won't be able to change it significantly unless you find your father in the figurative sense. In other words, you have to come to terms with what it was like to be that lost son. Men unknowingly hold onto this feeling of loss, and it corrupts their best fatherly intentions.

Terry, for instance, is the son of a superachiever, the chief executive officer (CEO) of a large corporation. He could never measure up to his father's expectations. His father criticized him when he couldn't color within the lines, when he wasn't the star of his soccer team, and when his grades weren't A's. Terry remembers that in junior high he was taking an advanced math class, and it was his toughest subject. His father was unrelenting in his criticism of his B's and C's, but one day Terry proudly put a math paper with an A circled in red in his father's hands. His father looked, nodded, and said, "The A is fine, but it's only a start and won't mean anything unless you achieve this grade consistently."

Terry's lost boy originated in those moments. When he felt that he deserved praise, he received warnings. When he fell below expectations and needed support, he received criticism. It was as if his father had abandoned a crucial role at these times, and as Terry searched desperately for support and approval, he received nothing. From an emotional standpoint, his father was invisible. Terry is now the father of two boys, ages 7 and 10. With both of them—and especially with the older one—he has adopted a time bomb style. Although he is careful not to be overly critical and offers praise when praise is due, certain behaviors set him off. Whining especially ticks him off. Part of him recognizes the overreaction, but it's almost as if he can't help himself. Once his older son was frustrated trying to put together a model airplane and complained, "I can't do this; it's too hard," and Terry went over to the table where his son was working, grabbed the plane's parts, and hurled them violently across the room.

Terry's feeling of being a lost boy is awakened by his own sons. He becomes scared that he is not going to measure up in their eyes, that he won't be able to help them with whatever it is they're whining about. As a result, he reacts like a lost little boy, losing his temper because their whining throws him into the past. Deep inside, Terry is terrified that he won't be able to give them "A" advice, that he's going to let them down in some way. His anger effectively masks this terror for Terry. Only when Terry deals with the underlying feelings of being lost, though, will he become a better father to his own sons.

Nine Traits of Fatherless Sons

In Chapter 4 I talked about the four "negative" fathering styles and the importance of turning them into red flags that will help you to identify counterproductive behaviors. Another, more behavior-specific warning system involves the nine traits of fatherless sons. These are specific ways of acting both around your son and in other areas of life that suggest that you are still feeling lost and abandoned. When you become aware of each trait, it will make you vigilant for behaviors that are rooted in the past; you will think about whether you are acting appropriately in response to your son's word or deed or whether your behavior is related to something your father did. In the latter case, identifying the trait will give you a clue to discover how and why you were a lost son.

Examine the following nine traits, and use the tips provided to determine which one is most relevant to you as a father.

Shame

You feel defective, inadequate, and useless because why else would your father ignore you or run away from you? These feelings may surface when your son asks you a question for which you don't have an answer or when he asks you to participate in an activity in which you're not particularly skilled. They also may hover in the background, a nagging reminder that you are damaged goods.

Be aware that stress often magnifies these feelings; recognize that the more stress you are under, the more ashamed of yourself you are likely to feel. You have difficulty with intimacy because deep down inside you don't want people to see this "defective" part of you, the part you're ashamed of. As a result, you may keep your son at a distance, afraid that he'll discover this secret part of you.

When these feelings of shame well up, pin down the specific action causing them. Sometimes we do things for which we should feel ashamed. Many fathers, however, overreact wildly, and shame is an inappropriate response. When your son asks you the capital of Vermont and you don't know the answer, you should not feel defective or inadequate. Feeling this way is a warning sign that you are still a lost son. If you snap at your son for asking the question or withdraw emotionally after he asks it (depending on your fathering style), then the lost son is causing harm to your father-son relationship.

Hopelessness

This overwhelming feeling hits you in the chest like a 50-foot wave at particular times. You suddenly feel as if your life is over and something awful is going to happen. Impending doom is a chronic reaction to situations that don't merit this reaction. Your son may get a poor report card or his team may lose an important Little League game, and you react with panic and despair. It is also possible that you are terribly pessimistic about your son and his fate. You feel that he is doomed to fail in whatever activity he tries, even if he does well initially.

While hopeless situations exist in life, most of the time there are legitimate reasons to feel optimistic, especially when it relates to boys who have their whole lives in front of them. Examine your hopelessness not only for the cause but also for the depth of the emotion. We all panic at times, and we all feel pessimistic when things don't go well. This lost-son hopelessness, however, is far more powerful and all pervasive. A sense of doom is one way of describing it. At the same time, if you were asked to come up with a rational explanation for this feeling, you couldn't. If this feeling surfaces regularly, especially in interactions with your son, then acknowledge that it's an echo from being neglected, abused, or abandoned in the past.

Excessive Guilt

You feel responsible for everyone and everything in your life. If your son scrapes his knee or gets in a fight at school, you feel that it's your fault. You are unable to see that things sometimes are clearly out of your control and not related to you. It is extremely difficult for you to say "No" to people without feeling like you're a bad person for saying that, especially when you have to tell your son he can't do something or have something. Guilt runs your life.

This trait is a little trickier to identify than the previous two, in that we all feel guilty to a certain extent, especially when it comes to our children. Nonetheless, the lost-boy guilt is tied to an egotistical belief that you are responsible for everything bad that happens. If you are constantly chastising yourself for everything negative that happens in your son's life, then this is how you are reacting to being a fatherless son.

Inferiority

You don't feel adequate or competent for any given situation or challenge. Whether it's your career, your relationship with your wife, or your relationship with your son, you feel like a phony. You believe that you are not smart enough, strong enough, or responsible enough to be a good father, and this belief can become a self-fulfilling prophecy. If you believe yourself to be an incompetent loser as a father, your son will sense your lack of confidence in your interactions with him and not trust you.

Monitor yourself for feelings of incompetence. Do you always feel ill prepared to answer your son's questions? Are you certain that you are giving him wrong or misleading answers? Are you convinced that every other father you know is better at parenting than you are? It's quite likely that you had a superachiever father who was so harshly critical that it made you think he wanted nothing to do with you unless you could do things better. In this sense, he abandoned the incompetent and underperforming you. As an adult, this abandonment translates into a belief that you are not good enough as a father.

Overcompensation

This is the fallout from not having the proper male support, approval, and guidance growing up from your father. With those buried feelings of being lost and alone, you overcompensate with a macho mentality. Underneath the bravado, though, is the lost little boy of long ago. You may take on the style of the time bomb or superachiever father in order to overcompensate. In fact, you are intensely competitive with all men you encounter, not just your son. With your boy, though, you act tough, brag about your accomplishments, and generally let him know you've got it all together.

Watch how you deal with your son's accomplishments. When he tells you about a good grade he received in school, do you reflexively relate the good grades you received? When he shares some knowledge he gained from a school field trip, do you have to "top him" with your knowledge about the subject?

Anger

This is an easy one to identify. It is not garden variety anger but rage that is always simmering just below the surface. The rage bursts forth at unpredictable moments, and your outbursts scare you because you feel absolutely out of control and very violent. After these outbursts, you may experience some of the other traits, such as shame and guilt. Your rage is the temper tantrum of a little boy, a cry of frustration. It also helps you to hide your childhood wounds from yourself; it is your defense against being hurt again. The anger makes you feel powerful, as opposed to being the helpless lost child.

Observe the frequency and intensity of your expressions of anger. If you find yourself frequently flying off the handle when your son does something, and if you are scared by how angry you become, then it's a sign that this is your fatherless-son trait.

Addictive/Compulsive Behaviors

In order to properly keep the pain of being lost suppressed, substance abuse or any addiction works wonders. So too does any sort of obsessive behavior, from exercising religiously to following a rigid diet. Whether a compulsion or addiction, these activities block the scary feelings that threaten to make their way into consciousness. The ability to stay numb or become numb is never dismissed or questioned by fatherless sons. Staying numb is a survival tactic and therefore very difficult to give up. Men exhibiting this trait will create ways to stay numb and skip over their father and son issues for as long as possible.

Consider whether you act compulsively around your son or do a lot of drinking at home. Many fathers avoid contact with their sons by spending an overwhelming number of hours in the gym, at bars, or engaged in some other addictive/compulsive activity. Perhaps you spend most of your free time locked up in a workroom doing various projects but don't invite your son to participate. All this will create a wall not only between you and your lost-boy feelings but also between you and your son.

Lack of Energy

It takes a great deal of energy, time, and inner resources to keep your fatherless-boy feelings suppressed. This is why many fathers feel enervated and don't pursue careers or relationships with much vigor. They don't take the types of risks necessary to get ahead in careers or build strong relationships at home because they are wiped out from dealing with their inner demons.

Think about whether on your days off you tend to lie around on the couch watching television, choosing this option rather than playing with your son. Over time, you avoid many common father-son activities— going to playgrounds together, playing catch, working on puzzles, and playing games. Or rather, you participate as infrequently as possible.

Poor Relationships with Male Authority

Any authority can become the enemy if your fatherless issues are left unresolved. This is not limited to your boss but also involves social institutions such as the Internal Revenue Service, law enforcement personnel, and schoolteachers. This issue causes many fatherless sons to keep re-creating situations in which authority figures have to discipline them.

While you obviously don't view your son as a male authority figure, you frequently complain to him about the various men in your life. You may even avoid taking on an authority role with your son, choosing a passive style in which you rarely express any strong emotion with him. Think about whether you have problems with male authority figures and if you've disconnected emotionally so that you don't have to assume this role in your son's life.

Identifying the trait that describes you best as a father is a great first step toward finding yourself as an adult. While you may find that more than one of the traits is applicable to you, focus on the one that engenders the strongest emotional response. Trust your gut. The odds are that one particular description really hits home—it makes you anxious or even scared—and that's the one you need to pay attention to. Whatever trait describes you, it is a sign that you are mired in the past as a fatherless boy, and as you might expect, fatherless boys make lousy parents. By identifying the trait, though, you have given yourself a conduit into the past to deal with the hurt that lost boy suffered. The trait is a starting point for self-discovery, a way to come to terms with the hurt in the past and diminish the presence of this trait in your fathering behaviors.

The Prodigal Son Variation: Coming Home to Find Yourself

The process of moving from lost little boy to found father can be understood via the "prodigal son" story from the New Testament (Luke 15:11–32). It is about the power of acceptance, love, and connecting to your internal father.

A wealthy father has two sons, one of whom takes the money offered and runs to pursue a life of pleasure. This son goes broke after spending his entire inheritance and is lost both spiritually and secularly. He is forced to work in the fields with his hands, and during this period of labor, he realizes that he can apologize to his father for leaving the family and work in his father's fields. The son decides to put his past behind him and starts on his journey home. The father has been waiting years for his son's return, and when he arrives, he gives him a ring (power), a robe (position), and the fattened calf (support). The son is overwhelmed by his father's unconditional acceptance, love, and readiness to receive him back into the family. The gifts of power, position, and support from the father immediately transform the son's life and his experience of fatherhood.

The lost son does a number of things in order to return home. First, he realizes that his life isn't going in the direction he wants (awareness). Second, he comes up with a plan to reconcile himself with his family, father, and himself (action, responsibility). He starts walking home, and his father has never stopped watching for him or loving him. This warm welcome from the father is the event that changes his son's life. The son realizes that he has been given a second chance with his father and with his life. It is a gift that he will not waste this time. The prodigal son needed to lose everything and have his own cave experience to fully appreciate what he had.

I'm not going to belabor the symbolism of the tale. The point is that no matter what type of father you have been to your son, you get a second chance. If you gain awareness of why you've had difficulty as a father and implement a plan to take responsibility for your fathering, you too can return "home." You will no longer feel like a lost son if you take this journey. You've already started the process earlier, gaining awareness of your father's impact on the father you've become in your cave experience, as well as through the other exercises. Now, though, you need to become more aware of the particular trait that is a hallmark of your parenting. Whatever trait you have identified, do the following with it:

- Imagine that your father is with you, and ask him the following question: "What did you do or say that makes me feel so [name of trait]?"
- Imagine how you father might respond if he were completely honest and forthcoming. For instance, if your trait is hopelessness, he might say, "I made fun of all your dreams. I thought I was giving you a necessary dose of reality, but instead, I was making you believe that you were never going to succeed at anything you tried."
- Tell your father how alone, sad, scared, and lost this made you feel. Say it out loud or write it down, but express it in some way.
- Forgive your father for what he did, and accept responsibility for your own fathering actions. For instance: "I no longer blame you for my hopelessness in raising my own child. I'm a man now, not a lost boy, and I realize that I don't have to treat him as if his dreams were stupid."

Remember, this one exercise is part of a much larger process. Incrementally, it increases your awareness rather than magically transforming you into an ideal dad. Still, it should allow you to feel a little less lost and a little more in control of your fathering.

Position, Power, and Support

In the "prodigal son" story, the son receives position, power, and support, and these are the gifts you need to give yourself. This isn't about confronting your father and demanding that he take you back and give you as an adult what he failed to give you as a child. Instead, you need to restore these things to yourself. The real core issue is finding the loving, accepting, and nurturing father in your own heart and life experience.

To do so, take the following steps that will help you to transition from the lost boy to the found man:

1. Give Yourself Approval to Be a Father

In other words, affirm your position, recognize your power, and give yourself support. Many men don't think much about what it means to be a father, both for themselves and for their sons. Instead, they drift into the role, carrying the baggage of being a fatherless son with them. They have accepted their role without thinking about it, without considering the strengths they bring to it. In a very real sense, they are unprepared not just for the responsibilities of being a father but also for the issues from their past that surface when they become a father. The anger, guilt, lack of energy, hopelessness, and other traits that emerge blindside fathers and cause them to act in childlike ways toward their sons. In one sense, they don't approve of themselves as fathers. In the back of their minds they doubt whether they have the stuff it takes to be good fathers.

You need to discard these doubts and offer yourself approval. This means recognizing your strengths as an individual and how they translate into being a good father. Ask your wife or a good friend to enumerate your strengths. Do you have a good sense of humor? Are you kind? Are you a good teacher? Whatever your strengths are, recognize that they will benefit your son in innumerable ways. If you are a good teacher, you can help your son learn how to do well in school. If you are kind, you can help your son develop a humanistic perspective.

These strengths trump your weaknesses every time, as long as you are aware of your fatherless-son legacy and resolve to rise above it. Approve these strengths and think about what they might mean to your son. Make a list of how your strengths can translate into qualities that will benefit your son. Doing this will reaffirm your position and power as a father and will allow you to draw on this knowledge for support.

2. Allow Yourself to Grieve

You may have come to terms with being a fatherless son intellectually, but you may not have dealt with this loss emotionally. The grieving process provides you with a way to let go of the traumatic experiences of your youth. It doesn't matter that they took place many years ago; you can still grieve the loss you felt and move on.

It is generally agreed that the grieving process consists of the following stages: denial, anger, bargaining, depression, acceptance, and hope for the future. Typically, people become stuck in one of the early stages. Lost sons frequently are stuck in denial or anger. What you need to do is walk yourself through these stages. For instance, create a self-dialogue along the following lines:

Denial: For many years, I refused to believe that the way my father had raised me had done me any harm.

Anger: I'm furious with all the stupid things my father did when I was growing up and how rejected I felt.

Bargaining: I suppose the bad things he did are balanced with the good things, so I shouldn't complain.

Depression: When I think of how lost and alone I was as a kid, it makes me terribly sad.

Acceptance: I accept my father for who he was and that I don't have be the same type of father or influenced by him in any negative way.

Hope: I know that if I am a conscious father who respects the power of my role and knows my strengths and weaknesses, I can be a good father to my son.

As you create this self-dialogue, allow yourself to feel the emotions you are describing. Grieving needs to be done with the heart, not just the head. If you do this, it will help heal some of the wounds you suffered as a boy and, more important, prevent them from resurfacing now and in the future.

3. *Increase Your Capacity for Giving Approval, Empathy, and Love*

You can increase this capacity simply by focusing your attention on showing these qualities to your son. Fatherless sons don't focus on them for all sorts of irrational reasons: They think that displays of affection will turn their sons "soft" or that being overly approving will spoil their sons. Or they believe that there is something feminine about displays of approval, empathy, and love. In reality, they give your son emotional power, psychological insight, and wisdom. They are tools to handle the challenges of being a man in a tough world. They are tools that your father failed to give you—or at least failed to give you consistently and fully.

Increase your capacity by taking a little time at the beginning and end of each day to make a commitment to give your son approval, empathy, and love. One man I worked with used to go into his small son's room while he was still sleeping in the morning and, while he lay there asleep and vulnerable, make a silent promise that he would find a way that day to show him how much he cared about him and loved who he was.

This is really a matter of effort and will. Men naturally have an unlimited capacity of love for their sons, but you can only tap into this capacity if you approach it as a strong, compassionate man rather than as a fatherless boy.

4. Develop Emotional Fluency

This step takes practice. It's likely that you were raised by a father who was emotionally tongue-tied, and as a result, you never learned how to say how you felt. Instead, you held your feelings prisoner and suppressed them as you got older. Or you may have expressed these stifled feelings as rage.

As you raise your son, you need to be aware that it will be impossible to avoid emotional pain in your relationship with him. He's going to do things that make you angry, sad, and disappointed, and you're going to engender the same feelings in him. If, however, you develop a vocabulary around these feelings, you will avoid the pitched battles and silent fury that strain relationships.

Find a way to talk to your son with feeling but without hostility. Don't react to a mean or hurtful action on his part with the same behavior as you demonstrated when you were a boy when your father did something hurtful to you. Instead, make an effort to be understanding and supportive. Ask questions rather than make judgments. No matter what the situation is—or how angry you are at him—make an effort to exhibit one of the big three—love, empathy, or approval. Whatever your son has done, he is like the prodigal son wanting to return home after his anger has passed. Allow him back in.

5. Banish Your Father's Critical Voice

If you are like most fatherless men, you hear your father's voice in your head. It doesn't matter if he died long ago or if he wasn't around much of the time. If you're a fatherless son, you carry around the explicit or implicit criticism of who you are. Even if he was an absentee father, you can create what you imagined was his criticism of you: "I'm getting out of here; you're driving me crazy with all your demands on my time." If he was there, he probably criticized you for being sloppy, for being irresponsible, for being rude, and for a million other flaws.

You are going to hear this same voice as a father. When you think about talking with your son about a problem, that voice will say to you, "Who do you think you are? You don't have any special insights. If you don't have something intelligent to say, don't say it." Many times this voice will stop you from acting in a mature, appropriate way toward your son. You may not consciously hear your father's voice, but it's there nonetheless, affecting your actions.

While you may always hear this voice to some extent, don't give it decision-making status. When you are not sure if you should interact with your son in some way, assess whether it's because your father—or rather, that imaginary father's voice in your head—would dissuade you from doing so. Admittedly, this is a tough step to take because this voice is subtle and operating at times outside of conscious thought. Still, it helps to realize that this critical voice is in your head and that you must listen to your own voice.

Moving On: From Father to Son, Past to Present

Here and in earlier chapters I have attempted to help you clear the obstacles that prevent you from being the best possible father that you can be. Like most of the men I have worked with over the years, you want to be a great father. Your inability to achieve this goal isn't due to laziness, disinterest, or some sort of genetic flaw. Rather, things you experienced as a son hamper you as a father. Because these experiences can operate below the conscious level, you are at a disadvantage. You have the impulse to be a terrific dad, but your history as a son short-circuits this impulse. Trying to rise above your past is a complex endeavor, which is why I have provided a variety of exercises and approaches to help you. Not only do all these different activities reinforce one another and increase the odds that you will successfully come to terms with the emotional fallout of being a son, but they provide you with options. If you found one difficult to work with, you had alternatives to deal with the issues from your past.

With the past out of the way, you are ready to focus on the present. Many men want to hurry up and concentrate on issues of immediate concern: They have been having lots of fights with their sons, they don't know how to handle a particular father-son problem, or they are worried about the type of adolescent or young man their boys are becoming. If they don't first address the underlying issues from their past, however, they have great difficulty dealing with these immediate matters effectively.

If you have implemented at least some of the activities I have suggested, you are now ready to deal with these present issues. Let's start with creating a great father-son foundation when boys are young.

6

Forging a Connection from the Start

Fathers and Very Young Sons

"I rarely feed or hold or play with my six-month-old son. It just seems like that's something my wife is better suited for. Maybe it's just a guy thing. I don't remember if my father was this way with me when I was a baby, but he certainly never hugged me when I was a kid, so I suspect he didn't go in for the taking-care-of-the-baby routine."

Ron, age 42

RON'S APPROACH frustrated his wife, Amy, who didn't understand why her high-powered professional husband of eight years had suddenly gone into an emotional coma. Before Ari was born, Ron and Amy had a very strong emotional connection, and Ron was particularly open and affectionate. After his son's birth, Ron stopped participating in the family. At first Ron claimed that he didn't know why his behavior had changed since his son's birth. Gradually, though, he acknowledged to her that not only didn't his own father hug him, but "he never said he was proud of me or came to any of my games as a kid. We were never close. I will get close to Ari when he is older; it doesn't matter that much now."

This statement by Ron reveals his own emotional pain, which is causing him to miss the very opportunity and relationship he wanted with his father—connection and approval. Sons always need love now, not later, and this is true from the moment they are born. Ron is operating under the cultural misperception that fathers don't matter much in the early years of their sons' lives. A father's involvement with his son doesn't commence at any particular age or developmental stage—it begins with the pregnancy.

Traditionally, infancy and early childhood are perceived as a time when mothers are primarily involved with the raising and nurturing of their sons. Fathers have willfully passed up this task and have handed their sons to their mothers. As a result, the father-son relationship starts off on the wrong foot, and this early theme of noninvolvement recurs throughout the relationship. The first impression a son has of his father is his absence, and first impressions count.

Being Part of the Pregnancy

Ideally, fathers will start their involvement in the parenting process the moment their learn that their wives are pregnant. This may seem counterintuitive to many men who are not undergoing the physical changes their wives do in these nine months. Men, however, are affected psychologically and emotionally. They are anticipating, dreaming, and worrying about both their sons and their own capabilities as fathers. They are fretting over lifestyle changes and fantasizing about their sons growing up to become great scientists, athletes, and scholars. Although they don't change outwardly, inwardly all sorts of transformations are taking place.

Most men, unfortunately, aren't particularly eager to express their thoughts and feelings about these subjects. In fact, many times they decrease the amount of time they spend talking with their wife during her pregnancy, perhaps fearful of unearthing the fears and hopes of a father-to-be. The typical male avoidance of this life-changing event most often manifests itself in fatherless sons. They are the ones who struggle most with the underlying issues of becoming a father for the first time because the event triggers all sorts of unpleasant memories from their own childhood.

Ideally, the exercises you've done in previous chapters will enable you to move past these obstacles and participate immediately in your son's life. Not only do you want to get the relationship started properly, but you also want to create a connection immediately, one that you as

a father can feel when your son is in the womb and that you will naturally want to deepen after he is born. To help create this connection,
here are a few things you can do:

- Talk to your son when he's in the womb. According to various
  studies, babies recognize and react to their mothers' and fathers'
  voices, suggesting that this reaction is related to hearing these
  voices in the womb.
- Talk to your wife about the birth of your son and your hopes
  and fears. Don't suppress the former because they seem silly and
  the latter because they seem "unmanly." Talking about these
  issues with your wife will help to strengthen your relationship
  with her as well as prepare you for building a good relationship
  with your son.
- Go to doctor's appointments with your wife, Lamaze classes,
  and other baby-related activities. In other words, don't just talk
  about it—participate in it. Seeing your son in the ultrasound
  or being part of a class with other fathers makes impending
  fatherhood more real than it has been, forcing you to address
  subjects that you may have been avoiding when it was just a
  far-off concept.
- Keep a journal during these nine months. It may be easier to
  express your hopes and fears in written form rather than share
  them with your wife. It's also possible that even if you feel
  comfortable talking with your wife about some issues, you can go
  into greater depth in a private journal. This helps to facilitate a
  connection with your unborn son because you are thinking hard
  and deeply about issues that, if left unexamined, could serve as
  roadblocks to your relationship.

The First Two Years:
Developing Fatherly Instincts

It is never too early to begin holding, hugging, and talking to your son,
not to mention changing his diapers. Especially in the first 24 hours
after he's born, you have a golden opportunity to bond and connect

with him. There was a time not long ago when people thought that babies were born blind and unaware of their environment. Then in the late 1940s and early 1950s, a technology and research explosion occurred that gave child psychologists the tools they needed to examine and interpret the highly complex behaviors of babies. Today most parents know that babies do more than eat, sleep, and dirty their diapers during their first four months. Child development researchers have found that by the time they are three or four days old, babies can recognize smells, voices, and faces.

Babies aren't the only ones whose abilities have been grossly underestimated. Many parents and psychologists still assume that women much more so than men have an inherent sensitivity to infants. This incorrect assumption leads to mothers being the primary caregivers during their child's early years. Many fathers doubt their own ability to deal with the needs and developments of a newborn and hand the baby off to mom. Fathers then say that they can't wait for their son to become older so that they can get involved in his life. These beliefs and behaviors are *absolutely wrong.* No scientific evidence exists to bolster the maternal instinct argument, and no psychological evidence exists to support the notion that mothers are superior to fathers when it comes to parenting infants.

In fact, fathers who have the opportunity to see, hold, and react to their infants within 24 hours of their birth tend to be just like mothers, experiencing feelings of enthrallment and bonding (*American Journal of Orthopsychiatry* 44:520, 1974). Fathers, just like mothers, can develop intense feelings of attachment and a desire for intimacy with their newborn sons. These fathers report their fascination with the smallest facets of their sons' appearance, movements, and chattering.

When babies are born, they have no real preference for one parent over the other or for a natural over an adoptive, step, or foster father. According to infant attachment theory, babies simply like to be held and stimulated and don't seem to care who the holder/giver is as long as that person is sensitive to their needs. At this initial stage, infant boys can become equally attached to any person who is a consistent, stable source of comfort, attention, and stimulation. Babies do tend to develop a primary bond with their mothers, but this is so because mothers generally are much more involved in the care and feeding of their infants.

Fathers could very easily make the same infant-parent connection if they were willing to take the time to do so.

Therefore, take the time. To this end, here are 12 bonding activities you can implement when your son is between the ages of 0 and 2 years. Remember that your early behavioral patterns, habits, and actions become the substance of the father-son relationship. Your primary goal with your son at this age is to bond with him emotionally. Without this bond, your son may experience serious psychological problems later in life. Therefore, consider putting at least some of the following suggestions into action:

- *Make consistent physical contact with your son.* Babies thrive when they are held compared with babies who are left in their cribs for many hours a day. A boy always needs to be held by his father. Burp him and tickle him as ways to maintain this contact.
- *Carry your son as much as possible.* Take him for rides in the car, runs in the jogging stroller, and bike rides and walks with him in a backpack. Babies enjoy changes of scenery and fresh air. You aren't spoiling your son when you carry him frequently, and other cultures consider baby carrying mandatory for their survival.
- *Massage your son twice a day for at least five minutes.* This stimulation is excellent for his cognitive, social, and physical growth. Rub his back, feet, and body when you change his diapers. Babies love to be touched.
- *Jump up to take care of your crying son as often as your wife does.* Learn to change your son's diapers at least once a day, and carry him around at night if he is crying, singing songs to comfort him. This is an excellent chance for you and your son to become "buddies" on these late night excursions around the house.
- *Give your son a bath, and learn how to dress him.* Dressing your son is a great way to learn about his personality and preferences. Watch to see what clothes and colors he picks out.
- *Reserve at least 60 minutes a day to be alone with your son.* Make an effort to establish one-on-one time regularly, ensuring that bonding takes place.
- *Smile at your son, and make eye contact with him.* If your son is almost three months old or older, you will be rewarded with

a smile back. Eye contact is considered one of the primary ways humans make attachments to each other. Babies are no different.

- *Talk to your son.* Tell him your story. He may not understand what you're telling him, but he'll find your voice soothing, and it will build an emotional connection. In addition, you'll find that it connects you to him as you tell him about who you are, what you do for a living, and what you hope to accomplish with your life.

- *Become aware of your son's developing cognitive abilities and skills.* The more you know, the more you can encourage and stimulate these abilities. Reading baby books is an excellent way to watch his development. Babies love to be read to and look at the pictures, and his responses will tell you something about his intellect.

- *Don't expect your son to be quiet or a noncrying baby.* Babies cry, and our response to their crying can make it worse or better. Since babies can't talk, crying is their basic form of communication with us. There is always a reason for your son's crying; you can learn to tell what it means. This is a good first step at opening the channels of communication between you and your son.

- *Develop a routine and relationship style.* It is astonishing how early these patterns can form. Some fathers start playing a form of catch very early on. Others enjoy trading sounds—the dad sings, and his son makes a specific type of sound in response. In a very real way, you are forming a relationship with him, a way of being together.

- *Play games.* Boys love physical touch and roughhousing with their fathers; they enjoy tossing things back and forth. This kind of play helps a young boy to understand boundaries and limits for himself and others. Boys feel loved when they have physical playtime with their father.

These 12 ways of attaching will evolve over the years, but the habits established early on become the foundation of your future relationship. Ultimately, what these 12 activities create as a foundation is trust. These involving, hands-on behaviors will help your son to trust you now, and they will predispose him to trust you later in life.

Early Childhood—Willfulness

The second psychological stage in a child's development—between the ages of two and three years—is often referred to as *early childhood*. During this stage, you son learns to control his body, especially in relationship to cleanliness and mobility. It is toilet training time, along with learning to walk everywhere, run, hug parents, and hold onto toys and other objects. With all these new activities, your son is going to display some degree of stubbornness. This can be acted out by retaining his feces or eliminating them at will; he may snuggle up to his father or suddenly push him away; or he may be very excited about hoarding toys/objects or ruthlessly discard them all over the house. Everything is a new adventure for boys at this age.

This is also a time of constant contradictions, mood swings, and new physical behavior. Your son can be very stubborn one minute about not wearing a coat on a rainy day and the next minute be perfectly agreeable about getting into his car seat. He can express loving cooperation one minute and tearful resistance the next. Men need to understand that their sons aren't being ornery or hateful but rather are going through a predictable stage of life and adjust their behaviors toward their sons accordingly. Just as important, fathers need to recognize that these contradictory actions signal the major developmental crisis of this age: autonomy versus shame and doubt.

As your son stubbornly expresses his anal-urethral-muscular behavior (toilet training), he will find circumstances and boundaries that will inhibit some of his self-expression. Your son may be unintentionally shamed over having an accident in his brand new pants or for making a huge mess with his food. Remind yourself as you are spending time cleaning up the mess and are late for work that your son's actions are normal, and although you want to communicate to him that this isn't "civilized" behavior, you don't want to work yourself into a rage because you believe that he is doing these things to drive you crazy.

When you express your displeasure with the mess he made—setting necessary boundaries—you will raise doubts in his mind about his abilities and whether he can meet your standards. This stage in your son's life is a double-edged sword. You want your son to explore and learn about his world, his body, and his expanding group of friends and adults. Simultaneously, you must watch your son all the time or he might run into the street, pretend he is a tightrope walker, and walk out on a window ledge. This concern gives rise to the psychological conflict that all boys at two to three years of age face: autonomy versus shame and doubt.

If your son fails to develop an adequate degree of autonomy, he will have difficulty in the subsequent developmental stages. Creating trust is a great way you can help your son gain this autonomy. Conversely, if basic trust has not been well developed during infancy, then your son's attempts to gain control of his anal, urethral, and muscular organs (toilet training experience) during childhood will be met with shame and doubt. Shame is a feeling of self-consciousness, feeling defective, and the uncomfortable sense that you are being looked at. Doubt, on the other hand, is the feeling of not being certain, the feeling that something remains hidden and cannot be seen.

You want to foster a sense of autonomy and adventure in your son. This is the time in your son's life when he will learn to express his will, in the sense of free will and willpower. While this won't be a mature incarnation of willpower—two-year-olds can be maddeningly stubborn and willful—it will lay the groundwork for future development of the will. Therefore, you need to set boundaries without making them so confining that his ability to explore is diminished.

The following activities are designed to help fathers create an optimal balance between allowing autonomy and setting boundaries:

1. Take your son outside to a park or to any outdoor place where he can explore, play, and be allowed to wander around the area without your direct involvement. Jungle gyms are excellent toys for boys to master.
2. Plan 10 to 15 minutes extra in the schedule for getting him ready, going, or picking him up. This time cushion will benefit both of you greatly and minimize power struggles. Don't rush your son or always put yourself in a time crunch with him.
3. Set up weekly situations or circumstances where your son can climb, jump, walk, and run without your direct supervision. He needs free playtime with you as observer rather than participant. Boys love to be watched by their fathers; it fosters feelings of security.

4. Allow your son to play in the mud, dig holes, and get really dirty. He will do it whether you like it or not. Doing it with your permission builds autonomy, not shame. Get in the dirt with him and assist with the hole digging. Let him be the boss of the digging project.

5. Allow your son to help you with chores around the house. Boys love to be physical and act like they are grown-up men. Washing the car or watering the plants is a great activity for boys.

6. Encourage any activity that involves hand and eye coordination. For instance, allow him to pound wooden play blocks with a stick or smack a plastic hammer into plastic nails.

7. Allow your son to play in the water, whether it's the bath, the sprinkler, or the local pool. Obviously, you need to watch him carefully in these situations, but such situations are great for boys because at this age water is an adventurous medium.

8. Plan trips to the zoo, aquarium, petting zoo, wild animal park, or pet store. Touching and talking to animals and sea life is a great form of exploration.

9. Let your son fall down and get up without your immediate intervention. He will communicate if the fall was serious. Many times your son will look to see if you are watching and wait for your encouragement to get up.

10. Set up situations that expose your son to different physical environments. If you live near the beach, go to the mountains, the country, or the desert. Try to be creative and push yourself to get out of your regular weekend routine.

11. Take the initiative and set up play dates with other boys and their fathers. Boys like to be around men. This doesn't preclude your son's mother from setting up play dates, but you need to create regular "boys-fathers" environments.

12. Learn about your son's "meltdowns" so that you are better prepared when they occur. Expect your son to be irritable when he is tired, hungry, and out of his daily routine.

13. Reinforce your son's accomplishments and acts of autonomy. This includes toilet training, eating, getting dressed on his own, picking up his toys, and responding positively to your request that he "behave himself."

14. Allow your son to develop his own routine. He might want to eat off the same SpongeBob Squarepants plate every night or drink from his favorite Mickey Mouse cup. These types of behaviors help to confer a sense of autonomy.

15. Give your son permission to choose his favorite food two or three nights each week. Even if this food is something you frown upon, indulge him two or three nights and create a healthier menu for his other meals. This is a good opportunity to balance his autonomy with boundaries. Many times men won't become involved in "kitchen issues," but this is an ideal time for you to get involved. Food can be an area around which fathers and sons can bond.

16. Establish nonnegotiable areas. If everything is negotiable, your son will have little sense of where the boundaries are. Make it clear to him that certain actions—running into the street for a ball, talking to strangers, or hitting his sister with a plastic baseball bat—are forbidden.

17. Practice saying "No." Saying "No" isn't bad fathering; it's part of your boundary-setting responsibilities. Of course, you want to integrate a reasonable amount of yeses into conversations, but don't be afraid to say no when it's appropriate.

18. Limit your son's options. Don't give your son too many choices or options. It is prudent to keep choices to no more than three things (outfits to wear, videos to watch, where to have lunch, books to read or buy). Too many choices are overwhelming for boys, and overwhelmed boys are much more likely to feel doubt and shame.

Many of these 18 activities/guides can be used in the next developmental stage of your son's life. In this stage as well as the next, you are helping him lay the foundation for who he'll become.

Showtime-Play Age: Purpose

This is the developmental stage of four- and five-year-olds and their ever-increasing ability to move around and meet the world head-on. Boys at this age are vigorous and highly active with a developing sense of their world and how things work (school, family, siblings, rules, right and wrong). The conflict of initiative versus guilt becomes the dominant psychosocial crisis of the play-age stage. Just as you helped tilt the balance in favor of autonomy in the preceding stage, you want to help your son to embrace initiative here.

Initiative involves a boy's ability to be active and engaging with the environment around him. He is becoming more capable of understanding social relationships, rules of conduct, and classroom protocol and expanding his grasp of the world.

While you want to encourage initiative, you also need to confine it to a certain extent. If you don't, it may lead to chaos and a lack of moral principles. On the other hand, if you push your son too far in the other direction, he is going to feel overly guilty, which will make him compulsively moralistic or overly inhibited. This is also the stage where little boys want to marry their mothers and might feel guilty for such thoughts. These types of romantic, innocent sexual feelings or thoughts are normal and part of the new interests boys have at this stage. You should expect your son to express these unformed sexual thoughts and feelings to you, and you should not censure him for it.

The ongoing tension between initiative and guilt produces the basic personality strength of purpose. A five-year-old boy will play with a purpose, competing at games in order to win and purposefully pursuing goals. While before he may have played idly with toys, now he invents a purpose to his play. Boys at this stage become upset if they perceive that they are wrong or they have lost a game. Morality, too, becomes a major concern for boys. For this reason, they are invested in being "right" and insistent that other playmates follow their rules. They label behaviors as right and wrong, and cheating by a friend can catalyze a fight. Boys want to win at their games, but they also recognize the importance of playing by the rules. Fathers who can maintain the right tension between these two paradoxical requirements will contribute greatly to their sons' development.

Helping boys to understand the difference between right and wrong is part of your responsibility, but you need to be flexible in your interpretation and enforcement of these moral principles. If you take a black-or-white approach—if you insist that he never, ever lie and that he always apologize if he's done something wrong—you are going to push him toward feeling guilty and away from initiative. He needs to have room to make mistakes, to learn that there are moral shades of gray, and that he doesn't have to castigate himself for telling a little white lie.

To help your son gain initiative without feeling overly guilty, here are some things you can do:

- Encourage his participation in all types of games with both you and his friends. Because all boys like different types of games, experiment with the gamut—board games, sports, cards, and so on. Don't only focus on formal games; he may prefer informal contests where the rules are invented on the spot. He may prefer indoor to outdoor games. The key is to try a variety and see which ones command his interest. This is when he will take the initiative and play with purpose.

- Point out examples of right and wrong. As your son develops his sense of purpose, you also want him to apply his energy and desire to win for the right reasons. If you are watching a baseball game with him and a player is thrown out for using a corked bat, explain to him how the player broke the rules and why he is being punished. Don't shove a moral lecture down his throat. Instead, be opportunistic, watching for chances to explain simple morality in terms he can relate to.

- Be responsive to his questions, no matter how silly or nonsensical they may seem. At this age, your son will ask a million questions; his inquiries are part of his growing initiative. Don't stifle it by ignoring his questions or not taking them seriously. If he asks you, "Why can't I fly like Superman?" try giving him a rudimentary explanation about how birds fly or something related to his question. Even if he doesn't fully understand your answer, he'll see that you took him seriously and be encouraged to show more initiative.

- Pull lightly on the reins when he seems out of control. Boys usually spin out of control every so often, but you need to monitor frequency and degree. When he starts becoming uncontrollable—if he's often involved in fights with other boys, throwing temper tantrums when he loses, or breaking the rules in order to win—then you need to constrain him. Sometimes all it takes is a sharp word from you to let him know that he's gone too far. It may take a punishment, like a "time out" or rescinding a privilege. By intervening at the right time with the right gesture, you allow him to maintain his initiative but recognize that there are limits. Admittedly, it can be difficult to know when you've gone too far—or haven't gone far enough. All fathers make mistakes, but the two big mistakes you want to avoid are never intervening when he's out of control and becoming so harsh that he loses all initiative.

Hope Is the Legacy of Trust

In these early years, your primary responsibility boils down to fostering a sense of trust in your son. You start building this trust when your child is in the womb and continue through infancy. Trust isn't merely a matter of being there for your child—although this is obviously important—as much as it involves the type of relationship you forge. Child development researchers such as John Bowlby and Erik Erikson concur that the quality of relationship between infants and caretakers is more important for the child's ultimate welfare than the sheer quantity of time spent together or the nourishment given. It is the quality of time, connection, and emotional atmosphere between the baby boy and his father that has far-reaching implications later in life. Merely feeding your son and sitting him in front of the TV watching a "Barney" video for hours on end is not the type of interaction that builds trust. Instead, the activities suggested throughout this chapter do build trust.

Although it may not seem like it now, these trust-building activities are critical to your sons' future development. According to Erik Erikson, children who develop a feeling of trust have a much better chance of negotiating subsequent developmental crises and of realizing effective interpersonal relationships throughout their lives. Children who fail to develop a trusting relationship with their caretakers (father and mother) and their environment will be perennially plagued by doubt. The long-term effect is that your son will have difficulty finding a niche for himself as an adult.

I am not suggesting here that you should "baby" your son during these early years. Erikson makes it clear that too much trust causes a boy to become gullible, naive, and overly vulnerable. What I am advocating, however, is that you ensure that there is more trust than distrust in your son's early years. From the time your boy is born, he will experience discomfort, hunger, and pain, but he also will experience the alleviation of these problems. He will gain trust in you and his mother and your ability to help him eliminate or diminish these problems. After a period of time, he will expect that even when he's terribly hungry or not feeling well, he will soon be better. This is hope, and it is the payoff for all the trust you nurture.

Again, according to Erikson, when infants have little hope, they retreat from the outside world and begin the journey toward serious psychological disturbance (E. H. Erikson, *The Life Cycle Completed: A Review*. New York: Norton, 1982). Childhood and adult male depression can be traced back to this early breakdown of trust between a son and his father. One of the obvious signs that your son is thriving with a high degree of trust is the absence of withdrawal behavior and a lingering depressed mood. If you follow the emotional bonding and interaction activities I've suggested here, you will likely build an early trusting relationship with your son. This trust, in turn, will foster a hopeful perspective, facilitating the way he deals with the inevitable setbacks and disappointments that are part of every life stage, including the wild developmental period that comes next.

7

The Wild Middle Ground

Between Childhood and Adolescence

My ten-year-old son is a wild man. I'm always yelling at him. I hate to hear my voice after a while, because it seems to do no good until I blow up—and then we both feel bad. I don't want to be a Nazi, and at the same time I don't want him to think I'm a pushover. I want him to be a good boy, respectful— not a wild animal.

Carl, age 36

THE 6- TO 13-YEAR-old stage is when boys define themselves. These boys tend to adopt a violent, civilized, or passive approach to their peer group, family, and romantic relationships as part of defining who they are. Fathers can help shape boys' choices during these years, influencing whether they turn into civilized, morally responsible young men or bullies, victims, or other negative types. As these boys move toward adolescence and act like they don't care much about anyone or anything, though, they actually crave mastery over their behavior. Dads can help them achieve this objective.

One of the challenges to achieving self-control is expression of emotion. Some boys don't emote at all, whereas others express their feelings inappropriately. Fathers can play a key role in helping their boys learn about and express their emerging emotional intelligence. Without a father's involvement, this can be a difficult experience. Jerry, for instance, tended to cry easily, even at age 11. When he played baseball and made an error, the other boys would yell at him, and although he tried to hold back the tears, they would seep out of the corners of his eyes. His friends would rag him unmercifully, and after a while, they would try to find ways to make him cry, almost as if it were a sport within a sport. Jerry was fortunate to have a father who neither screamed at him to stop being a baby nor was a passive type whose style would have been to ignore these incidents. Jerry's dad was nonjudgmental about Jerry's tears; he didn't say that it was good to cry and tell him things like "You're such a sensitive soul" or try to "toughen him up." Instead, he asked what had happened to make him cry and what he was feeling at the time. Jerry explained to his father that he knew making an error wasn't really a big deal, but with everyone staring at him and knowing that his friend Mike was furious at him for dropping the ball, it seemed like he had done something terrible, and he couldn't think straight about it, so he started to cry. His father's nonjudgmental attitude allowed Jerry to talk about these experiences, and by the time he was 13, Jerry was not crying at minor mistakes.

Jerry had "mastered" his thoughts, feelings, and behaviors. From a psychological perspective, mastery is the learned ability to have self-control in all areas of life. These are the years when your son needs to learn mastery skills, such as impulse control, delayed gratification, and independent functioning. Your son won't naturally acquire mastery skills; you need to teach them to him. If you fail in this parenting task, you increase his vulnerability to drugs, drinking, and other antisocial behaviors in the coming years, as the following example illustrates.

When John was 10 and in fifth grade, he was having various behavioral problems, such as getting into fights and arguments with other kids at school. John's father, Richard, wasn't good at setting limits and rarely disciplined his son no matter what offense he committed. Richard, a busy professional, also was deeply involved in his career and was away from home a lot. Even when he was home, though, Richard often seemed a million miles away, his mind still engaged with a problem from work. By the time John was 13, his middle school expelled him for possession and sale of hallucinogenic drugs. Speaking about this experience and his father, John said, "I probably would have never experimented with acid, but my father never really ever spoke to me about the pitfalls of heavy drug use. Now I kind of wish that my dad had spoken up, I would probably be doing better in school and not be in so much trouble. I could have handled my drug use better, but I have never had much self-control."

Listening to his son, Richard's face revealed a mixture of reactions: anger, disappointment, and resignation. Neither Richard nor John knew what to do next or how to stop the cycle from spinning into even more dangerous territory. Richard said to his son, "I was very busy building my law practice when you were younger, just like my father did. I have never done a very good job at containing you; it always seemed like you just never wanted any direction from me. I was stupid and took your rejection as a form of self-control."

Richard must realize that his lack of input and direction in his son's life has contributed to the mess John is in; John, too, must learn to take responsibility for his own problems. Neither event will happen, however, until Richard recognizes that even though he made a mistake in the past, he doesn't have to compound this mistake in the future. Unfortunately, Richard operates under the same false assumption that plagues many dads whose sons are in this age group. They are convinced that their fathering role has diminished, that their sons no longer need them in the way they once did. As a result, they opt out of a role that is as important now as it was in earlier years.

This type of mistake is common during this developmental stage. Let's look at how to avoid this mistake and be a good father during the "wild" years.

The Discipline Dynamic: Learning How to Set Limits Fairly and Effectively

How do you "install" an internal control system within boys that allows them to practice self-discipline but that doesn't crush their spirit? How do you get boys to stop themselves before they do things that are hurtful or illegal but also allow them to release a certain amount of wild energy? How do you help them to navigate between mastery and inferiority, the tension-producing poles of this age group? These are tough questions for fathers, but they can look for guidance to the disciplinary structures set up within schools. For instance, go to an elementary school and see the strict parameters that are in place. The teacher is very aware of the need for consistent, clear-cut boundaries and consequences. Standing in line, raising your hand to speak, waiting your turn to get a drink of water, and other rules are strictly enforced. At the same time, elementary school students are allowed recess and other breaks to blow off steam and for "free play."

Between the ages of 6 and 13, your son needs a similar type of limit setting and structure in his nonschool life. Your goal is to help shape him into a civilized young man, into someone who behaves appropriately at home, with his friends, and in other settings. Your conscious involvement will temper the wild side of your son and allow him to develop a sense of internal self-control, respect, and responsibility. A civilized son, for instance, can be engaged in competitive team sports without having to kill his opponent.

Ideally, your fathering will help him to develop his own emotional and behavioral thermostat. In other words, you will assist him in creating an internal device that lets him know not to take a certain action because it is self-destructive and that it is okay to take a risk in another area because the risk falls within acceptable limits. With just the right amount of limit setting and structure, you can help your son to govern his behaviors so that he responds to stimuli in a civilized manner. This internal regulator is critical to boys at this age because they are under tremendous pressure to act like wild animals rather than rational, empathetic children. Outdated beliefs about manhood, such as being tough, still dictate boys' self-esteem and peer acceptance. For this reason, boys gravitate toward bullying behavior and mock emotionally sensitive boys. Boys who express too much emotion are called "gay" and are teased unmercifully, frequently resulting in social isolation and even depression. For many boys, it is preferable to act tough rather than subject themselves to this fate. Unfortunately, acting tough often translates into experimenting with alcohol and drugs, smoking cigarettes, acting out at school, and engaging in other negative behaviors.

Fortunately, you can use discipline to help your son create his own internal regulator that will keep these negative behaviors in check. This does not mean becoming a fierce disciplinarian. Instead, it involves learning how to use discipline at the right time and in the right way. It also means using it consistently. Here are eight ways to employ discipline and help your son learn to make the right choices at this age:

1. *Talk about what are—and what are not—acceptable behaviors.* Talk regularly with him about specific things he's done, and let him know what's okay and what's not okay. Explore if a certain

behavior is acceptable under certain circumstances and not others—for instance, fighting to defend yourself. Include in the discussion specific actions and attitudes of his friends. Let him see his behaviors within the context of that of his peers and understand what you approve of. Don't be subtle. If you think something he did was terrific, say so. If you find it offensive, communicate it clearly. Your consistent reactions to his and other kids' behaviors will raise his awareness of where the behavioral boundaries are. In providing him with these boundaries, make sure that you're judging his actions and not him. This isn't a semantical distinction. If you are always telling him that he's been "bad," you're going to hurt his self-esteem and make him defensive. On the other hand, if you communicate that a specific "action" is unacceptable, you focus his attention on what he did rather than who he is. Your son will find this approach more palatable and take your words to heart.

2. *Inform him of the consequences of crossing the line.* Even at age six, your son is able to understand that if he persists in inappropriate behavior, he will suffer the consequences. Don't be vague and tell him that if continues to hit Johnny, he's going to "be in a lot of trouble." Make it clear that he will have his television privileges taken away for a week. Talk about these consequences and why you feel that the punishment fits the "crime." Let him ask questions or protest if he feels that the consequences you have devised are too harsh. This discussion will help to make him more aware of where the boundaries are.

3. *Enforce consequences when you are calm.* Consistency and logic should inform all your disciplinary actions. If your son does something that upsets you and you immediately implement a punishment, it is likely to be unfair and inconsistent with past punishments. If you son smacks his sister and you scream at him, "No Game Boy for an entire year!" you are creating a consequence you probably will not enforce, and you will lose credibility with your son. If you do enforce it, then he'll view you as being unfair. Wait until you've calmed down so that you can formulate appropriate responses to his negative behaviors.

The punishment should fit the crime. Boys need to differentiate between merely shoving another child and beating him up. They need to recognize what's really harmful behavior and what's only moderately objectionable. In this way, they can concentrate on moderating behaviors that elicit the severest consequences.

4. *Establish boundaries at home.* What chores does he have to do on the weekend before he can go out to play? How many hours of television can he watch each night? If he doesn't eat all his dinner, can he still have dessert? Establishing these boundaries isn't a sign that you distrust your son. Although he may grouse about the limits you set, beneath the grousing, he wants these emotional fences. They communicate your concern, support, and involvement in his life. Once you establish the precedent of setting home boundaries, it is much easier to expand the boundaries to outside the home, a growing necessity as he approaches adolescence. Remember, discipline begins at home.

5. *Give your son choices.* If you issue commandments as a way of enforcing discipline, you will create a boy who chafes under your rigid rules. Although he may obey you as long as you are watching him, away from your gaze he may revert to his "wild animal" pose. Bullies often come from homes where their fathers ordered them around. By giving your son choices about how and when to observe your boundaries, you empower him. This sense of power adds to his feelings of mastery over his environment. Rather than telling him that he can only watch one hour of television each night, inform him that he has a seven-hour "budget" for the week, and if he wants, he can watch four hours one night, three hours the next, and no television for the other five nights.

6. *Use repetition.* This is just another way of helping you appear consistent in his eyes. Repeat the limits you are setting at different times in different situations. If one rule is "no leaving the dinner table until everyone in the family is done eating," mention it at the start of various meals, and say it in different ways.

7. *Try to pay attention more and punish less.* During this stage, your son wants your undivided attention, and bad behavior is a ploy

to get it. Expect him to create situations that he knows will upset you in order to involve you intellectually and emotionally in his life. While there will be times when punishment is appropriate, you should attempt to spend more time with him and see if this moderates his "cries for attention."

8. *Don't get into debates when he has clearly violated established boundaries.* Earlier I advocated father-son discussions about boundaries, but I am not advocating allowing kids to draw you into manipulative debates. Some "soft-hearted" dads will allow their sons to rope them into long-winded discussions that circle endlessly—a boy's rationalizations for his behaviors often come into play here. When you start debating the merits of his violation, you are playing right into his hand. If he wants your attention, a debate is another way of getting it. In addition, these debates tend to buffer the impact of his negative behavior. After talking for a while, he may convince you to lessen his punishment, or your anger at him might diminish. Thus he loses the cause-and-effect lesson that you are attempting to teach him.

Finally, recognize that now is the time to establish discipline. Too many fathers wait until their sons are adolescents, and as the saying goes, by that time the horse is out of the barn. If you decide to tell your 15-year-old son for the first time in his life that you are implementing a curfew, he'll respond, "Why now? I never had a curfew before." And he's right. You are setting a precedent too late in the game. The preadolescent stage is when your son is ready and secretly desirous of the rules you lay down. He may tell you that you are being unfair or harsh, but this reaction is nothing compared with how he will react if you delay this disciplinary approach.

Creating Alternatives to Physical and Verbal Abuse

This is the age when your son will drive you nuts with his out-of-control behavior. There are going to be instances when he does something so stupid or offensive that your first impulse will be to lash out at him. Lashing out may involve a verbal threat, or it may mean giving him a spanking. You may be continuing a tradition of physical abuse that has been passed on from your grandfather to his father to you, such as beatings with a belt or an open-handed slap to the face. Or you may be carrying on a verbal abuse tradition, one in which you eviscerate your son in emotionally painful ways.

Whatever form the abuse takes, I can guarantee you one thing: *It doesn't work!* Excuse the italics, but this is a difficult point for many fathers to accept. Perhaps this is so because they subscribe to the "spare the rod and spoil the child" philosophy or because they don't see the harm in "good, old-fashioned discipline." Or they may believe in using "limited" physical punishment for egregious sins because it "seems" to work. Fathers notice that their boys are better behaved in the wake of the beating or that they avoid getting in fights at school or stop whatever actions catalyzed the punishment. Sooner or later, however, the boys will return to their out-of-control behaviors or do something even worse. Just as significantly, establishing a pattern of physical or verbal abuse now will cause serious problems later.

To avoid resorting to verbal and physical threats consistently, you need alternative ways of dealing with your son in these difficult situations. I will provide you with a list of alternatives, but first I want to emphasize the dangers to your son and to the father-son relationship of repeated physical and verbal punishment:

- *Intimidation leads to dysfunction.* When beatings, fear, intimidation, and physical force are the primary tools with which you discipline your son, you have greatly increased the odds of creating a dysfunctional young man. As an adolescent, he is likely to be withdrawn or abusive to others, two common reactions to the punishment he endured between the ages of 6 and 13. Discipline should be guided by love, respect, and support, and this is not possible if it is implemented in abusive ways.
- *Physical abuse turns boys into savages.* Boys won't become civilized if they are treated in an uncivil fashion. Many dads I have talked to don't view themselves as abusive. Instead, they see the "rare" spanking or slap as a way of keeping their sons in line. Or they admit that they don't believe in physical punishment but that their sons make them so angry and frustrated that every so often they

reflexively smack them. These outbursts teach boys the wrong lesson. Many times a spanking is ironic, in that the father is physically punishing his son for fighting at school or bullying a smaller child. If your goal is to raise a son who has the self-control of most civilized human beings, a smack upside the head won't accomplish this goal.

- *Spanking and screaming often reward bad behavior.* Most men are not child abusers who derive sadistic pleasure from hurting their sons. Instead, they are basically good people who just "lose it." As a result, they usually follow their physical or verbal abuse by hugging their sons or begging for their forgiveness. This sends a mixed message that only confuses their sons and often ends up encouraging them to repeat whatever bad behavior got them in trouble in the first place. Typically, these boys are hungry for their fathers' attention, and abuse followed by hugs is better than no attention at all.

- *Abuse can be a legacy passed down through the generations.* Studies indicate that 30 percent of men who were abused by their fathers end up physically abusing their own sons. If you are trapped in this cycle, the work in earlier chapters should help you to break it. Be aware that this is a vulnerable area for you. You also should be aware, however, that you may have reacted to beatings by your father by avoiding disciplining your son in any way. You are so terrified by that dark side of your history—the fear of losing control—that you hand off all disciplinary measures to your wife. As a result, you fail in your role as empathetic disciplinarian.

- *Threats breed fear and insecurity.* "I won't love you if you . . . " and "If you do that again, I'm going to tell everyone that . . . " are examples of emotionally devastating statements. While these threats may cause your son to stop his bad behavior temporarily, they have no effect on his future actions. Even worse, warning him that you are going to do something catastrophic such as withholding love plays havoc with his psyche. In his mind, he believes that your love is contingent on him acting a specific way, making it a very shaky love indeed. Boys at this age need to feel secure that the love between themselves and their fathers is inviolate. Without this security, they are likely to embrace extreme behaviors.

Now that you are aware of the cost of physical and verbal abuse, consider the following alternatives when your son frustrates or angers you to the breaking point:

Call a time-out. Time-outs work well for both fathers and sons during this developmental stage. When you are in danger of overdisciplining him through word or deed, taking a 5- or 10-minute break often gives you the time and emotional space necessary to think through your next step rather than allowing your churning unconscious to dictate your actions. It also will help your son gain some mastery of his own impulses. Rather than say something to you that he will later regret, he has the opportunity to weigh his words. You are modeling the behavior of taking the finger off your "hot buttons," and he may realize that he too can adopt this behavior. This is exactly how he learns to regulate his responses to situations. When he takes a step back and considers his options, he learns the benefits of not acting impulsively.

Rehearse what you're going to say. In the heat of the moment, we say and do things that we later regret. You can bet that your 10-year-old son is going to do something that gets your blood boiling, but rather than just react, you need to rehearse. You can pretty much guess what he is likely to do, given his past actions: get in fights, pick on his baby brother, or get in trouble at school. Rather than blow your stack when you receive yet another phone call from his teacher informing you of his misdeeds, think about what you really want to say. For instance: "I'm really disappointed that you were rude to Ms Jones in school today. It makes me sad to think that not only do you not respect her but you also don't respect mom and me, since your behavior makes us look bad, like we don't care enough to raise you properly."

Concentrate on communicating actions, boundaries, and consequences. In other words, focus on helping your son understand that all his actions take place within boundaries and that if he violates these boundaries, he faces specific consequences. Instead of allowing your unproductive rage to dominate your reactions to your son, channel it into helping him to make the connection between his choices and their consequences. Explain how his decision to smoke cigarettes outside school had the consequence of his being suspended and being grounded, that he could have made other choices that wouldn't have resulted in these same consequences. Helping him to understand that he has the power of choice is providing him with a lesson that he needs to learn. Mastery over his own behavior is the critical learning during this development period, and dads can point out how their sons can achieve this mastery in a given situation.

In terms of this last point, Andrew is the 41-year-old dad of 12-year-old Jason. Jason is extremely bright—he's scored high on every standardized test he ever took—but he does poorly in school. This aggravates Andrew to the point that he's engaged in a number of screaming bouts with his son. Andrew, an executive vice president with a *Fortune* 100 company, has a superachiever parenting style and is furious that Jason is wasting his talent. Once, after Jason flunked a major math test, Andrew lost it and told Jason that if he kept on flunking, "You are going to end up a homeless bum drinking your dinner out of a paper bag." When Jason just snickered, Andrew grabbed him by the shoulders, shook him like a rag doll, and threw him down on the ground.

Frightened by his action, Andrew began exploring other ways of dealing with Jason's contempt for school. Eventually, he began engaging Jason in conversations about choices and consequences. After a few of these discussions, Jason insisted that his poor grades were because his teacher was "lousy at explaining things." Andrew agreed that he may indeed have a bad teacher, but the fact remained that his teacher's records clearly indicated that Jason failed to turn in almost 50 percent of his homework assignments. Andrew clearly spelled out the consequences of this action—that not only was Jason in danger of flunking the class and having to repeat it in summer school, but he also was not allowed to play his Game Boy on school nights until his grades improved. During their discussions, Andrew and Jason negotiated an agreement that if Jason were to finish the missing assignments, he would be allowed to play the Game Boy two nights a week and that if he were to receive a C or better in the course, he would have his gaming privileges fully restored. Not surprisingly, Jason quickly regained his privileges, and Andrew felt much better about disciplining his son with calm words and logic rather than his temper.

Two Scenarios: What Would You Do?

Let's try to put the lessons of dealing with this age group to work by suggesting two common scenarios that you might face and the right and wrong ways of dealing with them.

Scenario 1

You come home late from a hard day at work, and your wife confronts you the minute you walk in the door and tells you all the things your nine-year-old son, Tim, has done wrong. Since he arrived home from school, he has run through the house and accidentally knocked over and smashed a vase, he had a temper tantrum when your wife told him he could not have more than two cookies with his milk, and he deliberately kicked the dog when it got in his way. Which of the following is the right approach?

A. You find Tim in his room and ask him why he is in such a bad mood. He explains that they had a substitute teacher in school who picked on him; he adds that he didn't get picked on a team during recess, and he's also upset about that. You immediately feel sorry for him and console him; you remember being in similar situations when you were young. You decide not to address his unruly behavior, figuring he's had enough angst for one day.

B. You immediately go to Tim's room and let him know that he's not allowed to act rudely to his mother and hurt the dog. You make an effort to keep your voice under control, but when Tim rolls his eyes and then turns away from you while you're still talking, you start screaming to get his attention. You call him a "spoiled little snot" and tell him that he'll be lucky if his mother ever talks to him again.

C. You find Tim, and as soon as you see the defiant look on his face, you start to lose it. But you are aware how vulnerable you are to losing it, so you tell Tim that you are going out on the porch for 10 minutes and that you will be back to talk him about what happened today at that point. When you return, you have calmed down, and it is clear that by making an appointment with your son, you have caused him to think about things. He immediately starts to offer excuses for his behavior, but you hold up your hand and say that you are not interested in excuses. You explain that the consequence of acting like a two-year-old is not being able to go out of the house to play with friends on Saturday and that if this behavior happens again, he will lose his outdoor privileges for the following Saturday. You explain that there are certain lines that aren't crossed in your house, and acting rudely to mom and kicking the dog are two of those lines.

The correct answer is C. This was a perfect situation for a time-out. Dad was tired after a long, hard day at work, and he was primed for an explosion. Recognizing that he needed a time-out—and that his son could benefit from one as well—he took a break and gave himself the space he needed so that he could talk calmly and logically with Tim.

Scenario 2

Your 11-year-old son, Greg, is fine at home but constantly in trouble at school. You and your wife have been called to the principal's office three times in two months, and when the fourth call comes, you've reached your limit. You can't understand why Greg is such a great kid when he's at home but becomes a monster in school, and when you make this point to your wife, she sarcastically says, "How would you know; you've been home one week a month for the past year." It's true that you've had to travel a lot for work, but still, Greg seems so happy and respectful when you've observed him. You've talked to him about his school behavior, and he's offered a litany of excuses: School is boring, the teacher is unfair, and acting wild and goofy makes him popular with the other kids. Although Greg has promised to try to behave in the past, he never keeps his promise. Which of the following is the right approach?

A. When you get Greg home after the fourth incident, you grab him by his shirt, shake him, push him down, and slam the door of his room so hard that it sounds like a gunshot. You have never spanked him or physically punished him in any way, but now you have decided that you need to do something out of the ordinary to get through to him. Clearly, he's frightened by your behavior, and you are hoping that he will be scared into straightening up at school.

B. You take Greg for a long walk and try and rationalize with him. You tell him how you sometimes got in trouble when you were his age and that you understand why he acts out in school. But you add that you expect him to take more responsibility for his actions now that he's 11. When he asks you questions about the type of trouble you used to get in, you are more than willing to tell him, and he seems so interested in what you have to say that you are pretty sure that you are getting through to him. You decide not to punish him for his behavior but warn him that it is not to happen again.

C. You recognize that Greg's acting out may be an attempt to get your attention, that he resents your long absences and doesn't know how to articulate his feelings to you. You decide to make a commitment to be at home more and become more involved in Greg's life. You also realize that you haven't done a good job of defining limits for Greg and making the consequences clear and that this uncertainty may have encouraged him to test the vague boundaries he has created in his own mind. You therefore spell out for Greg what the limits are—including what you expect from him at school—and what will happen if he chooses to ignore these limits as he did earlier in the day.

Again, the correct answer is C. In the heat of the moment, though, this isn't always the obvious answer. It is easy to see how the dad in answer A could allow his fury to control his disciplining of Greg and how the father in B could be manipulated by Greg. To create happy endings to these scenarios, you need a certain amount of self-awareness that will tip you off about what's going on. Although as an uninvolved observer you may be able to connect Greg's behaviors at school with his father's absences, it is sometimes difficult to make this connection when you are caught up in the scenario. Just by thinking about the scenarios and practicing the methods described in this chapter, you will ratchet up your awareness and find it easier to spot how your actions are influencing your son's behaviors.

This awareness is especially important to create during this preadolescent period because once your son enters the teen years, these scenarios can become even wilder.

8

Conversation Starters

Seven Key Topics for Your 14-Year-Old Son

If my father had spoken to me about important things the way he did about college football, I don't think I would have felt so lost as a teenager.

Seth, age 24

I F YOU ARE LIKE most fathers of adolescent boys, you are shocked by how difficult they are to talk to at ages 13 or 14. At some point they start offering monosyllabic responses and rarely, if ever, ask you anything. Dinner conversations are strained, and you discover that they treat most of your questions as if you are a detective investigating a murder and they are the prime suspect. Over the years, I have heard men offer variations on the following statement: "I don't know what to talk about with my son, and I can't even get him to respond to me. We don't seem to have anything in common."

This is tremendously frustrating for fathers on two counts. First, they feel that their relationship with their son is suffering. Without an ongoing dialogue, the relationship feels forced and foreign. More than one dad has told me that he feels uncomfortable in his teenage son's presence. The connection dads desperately want with their sons seems strained or even broken. Second, fathers are frustrated because they feel that they have much to offer their sons but aren't able to pass on their wisdom. They've been there, done that, and want to offer what they've learned to their sons. Unfortunately, the moment dads say, "When I was your age, I . . . ," their boys' eyes glass over and not a word penetrates.

I don't have a miracle cure for the communication difficulties that afflict father-son relationships. I do, however, have some suggestions that I have found to help start dialogues about critical topics. Recognize, however, that these dialogues will require you to open up and reveal your vulnerabilities. This is not about assuming the role of perfect dad Ward Cleaver. If you want your son to open up to you, you can't stand in front of him lecturing. In many instances it is your confession of weakness and mistakes that will open your son's mouth and mind and lead to the connection you seek. I am also going to suggest that you make an effort to listen and ask as much as you talk and answer. The goal is a dialogue, not a lecture. You want to stimulate give and take, not just one or the other.

It is important to start this dialogue on the cusp of adolescence and continue it throughout your son's teenage years. Although it may appear that this is the worst time to try to engage your son in conversation, he is ready to talk about a number of key subjects. Granted, he doesn't seem to be ready, but if he can get past all his anger, embarrassment, and fear, he is primed to ask you questions and give you answers. Certain subjects are very much on his mind, and as his father, you are the most credible source of information around.

What to talk about and how to talk about it are the keys. Let me list the seven key topics, and then when we look at each topic in depth, I will provide some tips and techniques to catalyze meaningful discussions that ultimately will bring you closer and allow at least some of your hard-earned wisdom to sink in.

The Seven Topics

1. Women
2. Addictions
3. Spirituality
4. Hopes and dreams
5. Fear and failure
6. Money
7. Responsibility

Before addressing each of these topics, remember that the best discussions aren't necessarily ones where you reach agreement. Expect your son to express ideas and opinions that differ from your own, and keep in mind that different isn't the same as rejection or disrespect. In fact, if your son feels free to express his different opinion and isn't afraid of losing your love and support in the process, you are definitely doing something right.

Women

How can you talk about this topic with your son when you often feel that you don't understand the first thing about women? Despite how much you don't know or understand, you have a better handle on the subject than your 14-year-old son. If you have a good marriage, you have modeled the types of behaviors that will have a positive influence on your son regardless of what your discussions involve.

Opening a conversation with your son about women is actually much easier than addressing topics that he may have no interest in (e.g., politics) or that he is tired of talking about (e.g., bad grades). Boys are fascinated by girls, and your son will have a natural curiosity about everything from the birds and bees to dating protocols. Don't destroy this curiosity by delivering a lecture or providing an endless reminiscence about your dating experiences in high school. Instead, try to let discussions about the opposite sex emerge naturally. As convenient as it might be, don't expect your son to waltz into your study and say, "Dad, I really want to get your perspective on what girls are looking for in guys." In the real world, sons don't ask fathers these types of questions.

Nonetheless, if you are alert for the signs, you will notice when your son's natural curiosity about the topic is piqued. Specifically, watch for the following situations:

- A girl starts calling on the phone and asking for your son.
- Your son starts repeating the name of a specific girl in his discussions with you or your wife.
- He shows interest in a woman member of your family—probably a favorite aunt or a nonconforming relative—by asking questions about her.
- He becomes intrigued by some female pop culture figure—an actress, a singer, or an athlete.

- He expresses concern about some girl at school who has been dumped by her boyfriend, who the other kids make fun of, or who is going through a family crisis.

Take advantage of these situations by making casual comments about them to your son. Give him an opening to talk. For instance, after the girl calls on the phone, you might say to him, "Is that the same Emily who lives near the high school?" If he just nods and doesn't add anything, don't push him. Try the conversational gambit again after another phone call, varying your approach: "Somebody taught Emily manners. When she calls, she always says hello, Mr. Johnson, and then identifies herself." If you do this three or four times, you are likely to reach your son at least once when he's in the mood to talk about her. As long as you are alert to these situations, are casual in your remarks about them, and keep trying to use them as conversation starters, your son will respond eventually.

When your son is ready to talk, you need to figure out what to focus on and how to keep the conversation productive rather than destructive. When you talk with him about girls, you are dealing with a potentially sensitive subject. You don't want to embarrass him or allow a difference of opinion to escalate into a hostility-laden fight. Therefore, don't

- Give him the third degree about his new girlfriend—Where does she live, does she do well in school, or what jobs do her parents have?
- Make him sit through a repeat of the lecture he heard in health education class.
- Engage him in the sort of sex-related, guy-talk banter you might hear in the locker room.
- Give him your views on what's wrong with women in our society.

Your son is looking for someone to bounce his ideas off of as well as supply answers to questions he's been carrying around in his head. Take on your role by listening to him and by trying to communicate information as part of an ongoing dialogue. You don't need to have all the answers—when it comes to women, no man has all the answers—and should feel comfortable telling him, "I don't know."

Here are some of the issues around which father-son discussions should revolve:

- *Specific rules for how to act toward a woman.* If you don't have daughters, your son may view girls as creatures from another planet. He may be wondering what it is good to talk to girls about. He may be worrying that he has to change the way he acts and talks around girls. Although you may find some of his questions trivial or impossible to answer, the main thing is to communicate specific values about how to treat women. Emphasize the importance of respecting women, of treating them as equals, and of not stereotyping them. Remind him how you treat his mother and how you behave around women with whom you work. He will grasp that letting your values be your behavioral guide is a good idea.
- *Dating protocols, dilemmas, and decisions.* The danger for fathers here is acting like they know everything there is to know about the art of dating. There is nothing sons hate more than dads who dwell on their own dating triumphs and expertise. Your son will come to you if he is upset because a girl he likes turned him down for a date or because he can't muster the courage to ask someone out. Don't try to "solve" these problems. Instead, let him get his fears and worries out in the open. This will do him a world of good and allow you to communicate about emotions rather than just the news of the day. It's great if you can offer him some suggestions about how to ask someone out, but don't feel like you have to be one of those talk show gurus who have all the answers.
- *Sexuality.* I am not going to tell you what you should talk about with your son regarding such issues as unprotected sex, sexually transmitted diseases, abortion, and the like. I will tell you, however, that nothing you say is going to have much of an impact if it is delivered as a cautionary lecture. Instead, you need to find natural segues to this topic. Perhaps your son informs you that a girl from his school has dropped out because she is pregnant. Maybe you watch a movie together that addresses the issue of AIDS. Whatever takes you to this topic, move into the discussion slowly and tentatively. Don't scare him off with dire warnings about unprotected sex or a rant about sexually promiscuous teenagers. Let a conversation develop from his questions, if possible.

- *Becoming a woman's friend.* Invariably, a girl will tell your son that she "just wants to be friends." Or your son will express this sentiment to a girl. In either case, boys need to understand that every male-female relationship doesn't have to be sexual; that they should value relationships with girls for their own sake. If you have a female friend, you should bring this up in conversation, reminding your son of this reality. Your son may want to talk about how when someone of the opposite sex says she just wants to be your friend, it's a form of rejection. You should raise the possibility that it is also an expression of caring.
- *Communicating effectively with a woman.* At this age, boys often feel that they are too ugly, shy, unathletic, short, or unpopular to be of interest to girls. When your son expresses this sentiment, it is a great opportunity to reveal a "secret": Women of all ages feel that communication is more valuable than great looks, money, and popularity. Men who have the capacity to articulate their feelings, thoughts, and ideas are very appealing to women. Men who actively listen to what women have to say are also appealing. You'll be surprised how grateful your son will be if sharing this secret helps him forge better relationships with girls.

Addictions

This is the time when your son will be drawn to various addictions—cigarette smoking, drinking, drugs, and so on. Many boys experiment with these things during their teenage years, and you may not be able to prevent this experimentation. You can, however, have discussions about these addictions that might dissuade him from falling into addictive patterns.

You are most likely to have a discussion about this subject when you catch him smoking, drinking, or using drugs—or when someone else catches him. At that point, you obviously should reinforce the notion of boundaries and consequences. However, this is also a good time to help him understand that kids who do these things aren't "cool" but rather are highly anxious teenagers who can't handle their anxious feelings. As a result, they adopt behaviors that numb them to their feelings. Smoking, for instance, has a calming effect, even though nothing has happened in the smoker's life to justify a feeling of calmness. It is simply an artificial feeling that relieves the anxiety. Boys are especially prone to these anxiety-relieving addictions because they don't know how to handle their fears in an adult manner. Lacking the ability to talk about their feelings and insights about their behaviors, they become enmeshed in these bad habits.

Explaining all this to your son may help. It certainly will communicate that smoking and drinking aren't the habits of cool kids but rather of highly anxious boys. This takes some of the romance out of smoking on the corner or drinking in the park after dark.

This is also a good topic area for story exchanges. Your son may approach you with a story about a friend of his who got caught smoking and was expelled. Return his story with one of your own. Perhaps you also were expelled from school for smoking when you were a kid. Or maybe you know an adult friend who has been in a treatment program for drugs, and you can share his experiences with your son. Stories about people who couldn't handle their uncomfortable feelings and turned to addictive behaviors provide easy ways of communicating for fathers and sons. Ideally, your son will develop coping skills to deal with these feelings because you have created an environment in which he feels free to express his emotions. Also, if you have helped him to develop an internal mechanism to regulate his behaviors, these addictions are less likely to ensnare him.

What you should be careful of, however, is glamorizing your own drug or drinking history. To ingratiate yourself with your son you may tell him tales of how you went through college in a marijuana haze or how you used to consume a six-pack a night routinely when you were his age. You may have a lot of humorous stories from your youth about drugs or drinking that you believe he'll appreciate, and they may be highly entertaining. Be careful, however, if the message you're sending is that there's nothing wrong with drinking or using drugs to excess, because *you did it and you turned out fine.* This may not be your intended message, but it's likely the one he'll take away from these types of stories. Therefore, make sure to communicate the negative consequences of your addictive behaviors: a flunked test, the loss of a girlfriend, a missed job opportunity. If there were no negative consequences—if it's just a story about what a wild and crazy guy you were in your youth—don't tell it.

Spirituality

I am defining spirituality in the broadest possible sense here. Boys generally don't talk about spirituality per se, but they are thinking about their purpose in life, what life means, and the idea of God. Even if you haven't raised them to be religious, you will find that they are contemplating death and the afterlife and their own personal beliefs about heaven and hell.

Admittedly, you may find that your son is reluctant to talk about these issues with you initially. Unlike the previous two topics, this one isn't concrete. Therefore, you need to find a way to anchor your discussion in a specific event. If you just ask your son point blank, "Do you believe in God?" you are going to get a shrug or a disdainful glance. If, however, you take him to church after a terrible national tragedy and the sermon is entitled, "How Can God Let These Things Happen?" you are much more likely to have a productive discussion. It is not necessary to go to church, though, to spark a discussion about spiritual matters. After the September 11 tragedy, CNN conducted a survey that asked, "Do you believe in God?" and 93 percent of Americans said, "Yes." Just watching the news and seeing these survey results could provide an opportunity for discussion.

Perhaps the most powerful conversational stimulus, though, involves the death of someone you know and care about. After attending the funeral with you, your son may be in the mood to talk about the notion of a meaningful life or talk about a belief in a higher power. One of the best ways you can motivate your son to engage in this dialogue is being honest about your own feelings and beliefs. For instance, if someone close to you dies, you might say, "Whenever this happens, I wonder how God can let someone who is such a good person die when all these bad people are allowed to live to be much older than my friend." Your son will appreciate your honesty of expression and resonate to your sadness, and he may respond with a similar expression of feeling.

Spiritual discussions are truly important for boys in a volatile, complex world. It is so easy for them to become prematurely cynical and pessimistic, to view life as meaningless and believe that it doesn't matter what they do because there's no point to it all. This sad philosophy gives them license to be self-destructive and cruel. When there is no point to life, society's rules and regulations—not to mention the boundaries you have set out for him—can be easily ignored.

You can't "make" your son develop a spiritual side through conversation, but you can give him nudges in that direction. Maybe something you say will spark his interest in meditation. You might engage him in a debate about whether God is dead that will cause him to start reading books about religion. Ultimately, your talks may help him to recognize that there is something bigger than himself out there. Teenage boys tend to view their world within narrow parameters. When they start realizing that there are more important things than getting a new CD or being invited to a certain party, they become more civilized human beings.

Hopes and Dreams

Many father-son conversations revolve around disappointments and defeats rather than hopes and dreams. You end up spending a disproportionate amount of talk time chastising your son for poor grades, getting in trouble, or falling short of expectations in some other way. Allowing your son to express his hopes and dreams to you—and believe me, he has them, even though he may not readily admit it—is the type of experience that can bring you closer. Sharing a dream is a sign of trust. If he allows you to view his secret hope, he is making himself vulnerable to you; it means that he trusts that you won't mock or dismiss this part of himself.

Your son may never have expressed what he longs to achieve because he is embarrassed by what he perceives to be an impossible dream. Or he may be reluctant to articulate it because he feels you won't take his dream seriously. Or it may simply be that you haven't given him the opportunity to talk about it. Fortunately, encouraging conversations of this type is relatively easy. Here are some ways you can help him talk about his dreams:

- *Take him some place out of the ordinary*—a camping trip, a weekend in another city, or a hike in the woods—where you will have time alone and be in a "foreign" environment where he might not feel so constrained. Share your dreams with him, whether they have been realized or not. Tell him what you yearned for when you were his age and what your current wishes are. If you didn't fulfill your dreams, let him know how that feels. Be honest. The odds are that he will reciprocate. He might not tell you everything that he hopes for, but he may let you in on some small piece of what he sees himself doing or being in the future.

- *Coach your son on the process of fulfilling a dream.* You don't have to be a coach or a therapist to do this. It is simply a matter of drawing on your own experience and remembering how you achieved an important goal. If you think about it, you will recall that you visualized this goal, created a plan to achieve it, and found a way to work around obstacles that stood in your way. As you are talking with your son, see if you can direct the conversation to these three areas—visualizing his dream, a general plan to achieve it, and obstacles that might stop him. It is also great if you can talk to him about what happens when you fall short of a dream and how that is disappointing but often leads you in a new direction.

- *Do a "dream exercise" with your son.* Both you and your son should create a written list of all the things you want to do or achieve in your life. Each of you should do the list separately and then compare your results. You can put anything you would like on the list, from financial achievements to jobs to travel to relationships to hobbies. List as many things as you would like. Don't limit yourself to "realistic" goals such as graduating college or becoming your company's vice president. Include real dreams, such as sailing around the world or working as a missionary in a third-world country. When you are done, exchange lists and talk about what you listed. As you will discover, there's a lot to talk about.

Fear and Failure

No matter how self-confident your son may seem or how successful he is at school or sports, he has a place inside him where he is afraid. This fear has been with him always, and he may well have talked to you about it when he was little: "Daddy, I'm afraid there's something in the closet." Talking about it then helped to diminish his fear. Now, though, the fear is pushed deeper down and is more subtle. Many times boys on the cusp of adolescence are most afraid of failing in any one of a thousand ways. It is the ugly fear of being less than or not enough because he might not get straight A's or because he might strike out with the bases loaded. Adolescents magnify failure in their mind's eye, unable to put a bad grade or a bad swing in perspective. From their view, this failure seems like the end of the world, and it makes them afraid, sometimes to the point that they don't want to take any risks where they might fail.

Your conversations around this subject should communicate to your son that while it is natural to fear failure, it is okay to fail. There are going to be teachable moments in your son's life when he's ready to listen to you and to talk about his fear. At certain times, though, he will steadfastly deny that he is afraid, especially if you are a superachiever or time bomb father. He probably won't want to let the former down or anger the latter with his admission of fear. Still, he will reach a point where he's ready to talk about it, and you need to be alert for that moment. Typically, it occurs after a failure. In the wake of a bad grade or being turned down for a date, he may make a statement expressing his unwillingness to take a similar risk in the future. For instance:

- I'm never going to take an honors class like that again.
- Next time I ask a girl out, I'm going to be sure that she wants to go out with me.
- I'm not trying out for the newspaper next year; the system is fixed.

When you hear these risk-averse statements, you have a teachable moment in front of you. Don't ruin it by challenging your son and saying, "That's ridiculous; the system isn't fixed." Instead, tease out the reasons for his fear, and help him to analyze them logically. You also should share your own stories of how you have failed and why the experience wasn't fatal. Think about your own failures in the following four categories: school, relationships, sports, and career. Talk about how and why you failed and how it was a scary experience for you. At the same time, give him the benefit of hindsight. Looking back, where did each failure lead? Did it make you more resolute? Did it lead to an unexpected opportunity?

Sports is a particularly rich conversation topic, especially if your son is interested in being on a high school team. Just about every athlete is afraid of messing up in a crucial moment—dropping a pass in the end zone, striking out with the bases loaded, or missing a last-second shot. In fact, even the best athletes usually experience this failure not just once but a number of times during their high school careers. It's also possible that your son wants to try out for a team in high school, but he's afraid of the humiliation of being cut or being put on the "B" team. He may say things like, "I'm not trying out for basketball because I don't have the time," but it may be that he's really afraid of what might happen if he does try out. The point here isn't to eliminate his fear or tell him how to cope with a sports-related failure. Instead, use his interest in sports and worries about failing at it as a way to engage in meaningful conversation with him.

The other thing you can do is to share the "focus and faith" method with your son as an antidote to fear and failure. No doubt during your discussion your son will harp on the difficulty he is having in a given area of his life and how hopeless he seems in this area. Try to shift his focus from the problem to the solution. Instead of talking about all the things that he said wrong when he asked a girl out on a date, ask him what he might say right. Role-play with him if he is up for it. Make a game of it, asking him to come up with a line or idea that would increase the odds that a specific girl would go out with him. Even if he comes up with ridiculous things that would never work, it will help to shift his thinking away from the problem and toward the solution.

You also should try to instill faith that things will work out. This is a tough job, in that he may have not had any experiences that justify this faith. Besides recalling your own rebound from failure, you might cite how other people you know have managed to overcome setbacks. What you want to do is build the case over time that failure isn't fatal.

Money

This is one of the easier subjects on the list for fathers and sons to discuss. In our culture, many men derive their self-worth from how much money they make and the quality and quantity of their possessions. Boys, too, are influenced by this culture, especially as it is communicated through advertising. In their minds, money equals happiness.

It's not that fathers should tell their sons that money is bad. Far from it. It is only bad when people use it to substitute for the deeper things they really need: love, spirituality, and fulfillment. You should convey to your son that money is great but that he needs to learn to manage it rather than allow it to manage him. Even in adolescence, dysfunctional money-management behaviors arise, the most common one being the kid who maxes out the credit card his parents give him. Later in life this dysfunction can take the form of being penurious or of being incapable of managing money.

Your discussions should help your son to put money issues in perspective. Try playing the "million-dollar money game" with your son by asking him the following questions:

- If I were to write you a check for a million dollars, what would you do with the money?
- Would you spend all the money, or would you save any of it?
- Would you think about giving any of it to charity; if so, which charities and why?
- If you had a million dollars, do you think all your problems would be solved? What problems might you still have despite the money? What new problems might you develop because of all that money?
- If you had a million dollars, how do you think your friends would treat you differently? Do you think it would be hard to tell who were your real friends and who were just sucking up to you because you were rich?

Invariably, these questions will lead to other questions. You will find that your son enjoys speculating about what he would do with the money, but usually early on in the discussion he will run out of things that he would buy for himself and turn his attention to money versus self-worth issues.

If you need further information about the psychological impact of money on adolescents, take a look at Jon and Eileen Gallo's excellent book *Silver Spoon Kids*.

Responsibility

Adolescent boys are notorious for making excuses, for blaming others, and for rationalizing why they didn't do what they said they were going to do. In short, they don't take personal responsibility for their actions. You can't talk your son into being responsible, but you can talk with your son about his areas of responsibility. This is an important discussion not only for now but also for later in your son's life. Irresponsible teenagers often become irresponsible adults. They grow up blaming others when things don't go their way, and they live in the past. They ascribe their failures or limited success to some event or individual in their past. They blame fathers, teachers, bosses, and other paternal figures for problems in their lives. As a result, they cede control of their lives to others.

To help your son avoid becoming this type of adult, you should talk about exactly what he is responsible for. Some common areas of responsibility include

- Grades
- Chores around the house
- Getting and keeping a summer job
- Being home by a certain time at night
- Attending specific family functions

Expect that your son will not fulfill some of these responsibilities. At this point it is time for a discussion. He probably will offer you all sorts of excuses and rationales for why he didn't live up to his responsibility. Don't let him get away with it. This is a topic where you need to challenge him, asking the sorts of questions that make him uncomfortable. If he tells you that he didn't make his bed because he was late for school, ask him why he didn't get up earlier. When he tells you that he didn't get up earlier because he was up late studying, ask him why he didn't plan better so that he could go to bed at a reasonable hour. Through this Socratic approach, you force him to examine his false assumptions about responsibility.

Your son isn't going to like these questions. It is much easier to blame others for your irresponsibility than to own up to it, especially when you are 14. You need to assess how much he can take before he blows up or tunes you out. Still, he has to learn that he can control his fate and that he is giving away his power when he makes excuses and offers rationalizations. Questioning his excuses will prompt him to think about issues of personal responsibility.

If the questioning doesn't work, you might also take a cue from Barry, the father of 15-year-old Derek. Derek was a serial excuse maker. Nothing was ever his fault. In a way, he was brilliantly creative about wriggling out of his responsibilities. When he lost a summer job at a fast-food restaurant, it was because his boss, Mr. Charles, had it in for him because Derek suggested some improvements to the way they processed orders. When Derek was suspended from school for fighting by Principal Crawford, Derek said that Principal Crawford automatically assumed that he was guilty because of a past incident. When Derek blew off an appointment with his therapist, Derek swore that he had arrived at the therapist's office but that the door was locked so he had come home.

Barry hit on an effective way to challenge Derek without getting in a no-win screaming match. He called up Mr. Charles, Principal Crawford, and the therapist and made appointments for him and Derek to see each of them and to "get to the bottom of these situations." He explained to Derek that they would meet with each person, and that if he had accused Derek unfairly of shirking his responsibilities, he would apologize. Not surprisingly, Derek didn't want to go to the meetings and grudgingly admitted that maybe he had been irresponsible.

Father-son discussions about personal responsibility can be painful, but it is better to have them at age 14 than to have your son blaming others for his problems when he's an adult.

The Value of Just Talking

These conversations allow you to pass on important information to your son and shape his beliefs and values at a critical juncture in his life. Although they should start around age 14, they are going to continue throughout his adolescence. Over time, some of your points will sink in. Through repetition, your modeling behaviors, and his own life experiences, he will "get" some of your points, which is terrific.

The other benefit of these conversations, though, is that you are establishing a connection with your son that goes beyond what is said. Many times, avoiding talking to your son seems infinitely preferable to hearing him speak to you sullenly, angrily, or spitefully. It is very easy to slip into a rut where you rarely discuss anything meaningful because neither of you wants to deal with the emotions simmering close to the surface. This is fine if you want to avoid fights, but you also are avoiding having a real relationship.

You want to get into the habit of having regular talks with your son at age 14 because the longer you delay, the more difficult it gets. Setting a precedent early on will make these conversations more natural for both of you. Ideally, they will become a reflexive response to problems and opportunities in his life. More important, they will provide the glue for the father-son relationship, allowing you to say things to each other than you can't say to any other men in your life.

9

The Terrible Teens

*How Dads and Sons Can Make It Through Adolescence
with Their Minds and Relationships Intact*

*I worry all the time about my 16-year-old son, Alex; he has had such an
explosive temper since he was a little boy. He gets so upset at times I don't
know what to do for him or with him.*

Alan, age 57

There are probably more challenging tasks than being a father
to a teenaged boy, but off the top of my head, I'm not sure I could
name them. All a father's doubts and fears and all a son's hostility and
insecurity come boiling to the surface during this period. Too often
fathers and sons wage internecine battles that no one wins, engaging in
a series of raids and reprisals that leave both parties hurt.

It doesn't have to be this way. Or at least it doesn't have to be as bad
as it often gets. If you adhere to the suggestions for dealing with your
own wounds as a son and do the right things with your boy before he
reaches adolescence, you will stand a much better chance of enjoying a
mutually rewarding father-son relationship during this time. It also
helps if you know what to expect from your teenager and relate to him
in ways that facilitate the maturation process.

We will examine what you can expect and the specific things you
can do to help your son through this passage to adulthood. First,
though, we need to look at the worst-case scenario.

Prepare for the Worst, Hope for the Best

Be prepared to deal with a boy who acts in ways that can be disturbing and worrisome. For some men it is a shock to see their adorable little boy transformed into a hormonally addled teenager. Teenaged boys can be amazingly sullen, hostile, withdrawn, and anxious—sometimes all these things within a 24-hour period, or so it seems. Ideally, your son will have a minimal number of mood swings and generally be a good, relatively even-tempered kid. Even in this ideal case, however, you need to be ready for some outbursts and obnoxious behavior. To prepare you for the worst, let's look at what really is the worst possible scenario for adolescent boys and the psychology behind this scenario.

Eric Harris and Dylan Klebold, the two teenagers who were responsible for the shootings at Colorado's Columbine High School, epitomize the nightmare of male adolescence. These boys represent the worst fears of fathers. It is not that every father expects his son to cross the line and become a murderer. It is that all fathers know the volatile moods of their teenage boys and worry that their sons will do something stupid that they will regret the next day—or for the rest of their lives. It could be anything from driving drunk to having unprotected sex to striking a teacher to dropping out of school.

Shortly after Columbine, Alan called, worrying that his son had the potential to be violent. He referred to a few incidents in the past year in which his son had become angry—he had used a profanity when arguing with his mother and, after an argument with his father, had slammed a door so hard the glass window in the door had shattered. As we talked and Alan expressed his concerns, I jokingly asked Alan if he would know if his son had a weapon hidden in his room or was building a bomb. Alan, though, took the question seriously and said, "Yes, absolutely, I am in Alex's bedroom all the time, listening, talking to him, and watching him. He knows I am very interested in his life. I am always close to him."

I explained to Alan that the boys who get in real trouble are usually the ones who don't have anyone listening, talking to, or watching them. If he knows his son's friends, what he is doing most hours of the day and night, and how he is behaving and talking, then it is highly unlikely that his son will act violently or do anything that they both will regret for years to come. I also told Alan that if he is spending time with his son talking, listening, and being supportive, then he is giving his son something that boys who get in trouble generally don't receive. A father's neglect, avoidance, and denial are the catalysts for all sorts of adolescent problems. Boys whose fathers don't pay much attention to them, who don't spend much time with them, and who pretend that there's nothing wrong are the ones who act out. They may not shoot anyone, but they wreak havoc in their lives and the lives of their parents, and in the process, they damage the father-son relationship.

You can do a lot to prevent this from happening, and the first and most important thing to do is to become an active observer of and participant in your teenager's life.

Paying Attention to What Your Son Is Doing and Thinking

Mothers generally are much better than fathers at heeding the signs that something is wrong. Or rather, women tend to take antisocial behaviors seriously, whereas men tend to rationalize them, saying such things as, "I was just like that when I was his age." Dads who dismiss such things as excessive bullying behavior, use of alcohol and drugs, and emotional withdrawal usually are not very involved in their sons' lives. From a distance, it seems like they are just being typical adolescents. Up close, though, it is clear that they are experiencing problems and need someone— preferably dad—to intervene.

See if you can answer the following two questions that I ask every father to determine how aware he is of his son's activities and mind-set:

- On a scale of 1 to 10, can you accurately determine the intensity of your son's anger, violence potential, or hatred?
- Do you know where your son is, what he is doing, and who he is doing it with between the hours of 3:00 and 8:00 P.M.?

If you don't know the answers to these questions, you need to take the time and make the effort to find out. In terms of the first question, talk to your son as well as to his teachers and counselors at school to assess how close he is to the boiling point. While teenagers can exhibit other troublesome moods and behaviors besides anger-related ones, anger is often the easiest barometer to read. If you have a son who scores in the 7 to 10 range—your "guesstimate" based on what you have heard and observed—then you should be concerned. This is a clear sign that you have to become more involved in his life, that you have to become a better listener and communicator, and that you may need to bring a therapist into the picture.

The Washington, D.C.–based group Fight Crime reports that many of the serious problems, poor choices, and crimes boys get into occur between the hours of 3:00 and 8:00 P.M. Boys often do not know what to do with their free time, especially when their fathers and other adults aren't supervising them or setting limits. All adolescents are driven by the need to fit in and to be like everyone else, and if the norms involve drugs, drinking, and other antisocial activities, this five-hour period is when they are most likely to engage in these activities.

If you don't know where your son is during this period—and it doesn't count if you know where he is one day out of seven—then you must make a concerted effort to become more aware of your son's activities. This does not mean becoming Big Brother, but it does mean making a habit of talking to your son before he goes out and after he returns so that you know what's going on. It also means being alert for discrepancies between what he tells you and what common sense or other sources tell you about his activities. If he tells you that he is going to be at his friend Jeff's house, for instance, and you see Jeff with a group of other kids at the mall during this time, you need to confront your son about the discrepancy.

Finally, recognize how easy it is for adolescent boys to feel isolated and alone if you are not an integral part of their lives. Although every teenaged boy has moments when he feels alone and angry, the ones who have an involved father don't retreat to the periphery of groups. They participate in activities at school or pursue an interest outside school, have friends with good values, and generally are able to act in a civilized manner when family and other adults are around. They are not perfect and may go through some rough patches, but on the whole, they are doing fine.

Take Action When His Attitudes and Actions Are Disturbing

Now let me paint you a picture of the boy whose father isn't fulfilling his role. The father is a passive type, a time bomb, a superachiever, or absent. For whatever reason—probably having to do with his own dysfunctional relationship with his father—he is not paying attention or doing what he needs to do as a father. As a result, his son is the type of boy who feels left out of the family loop. He wonders who really cares about him. He feels out of place in his home, at school, with his peer group, and in the world at large. He is the same type of boy you see when you go to the mall; he's hanging out and staring idly, waiting for something to happen. He watches MTV and the worst shows on televisions for hours each week and spends an equal amount of time playing violent video games. He rides his skateboard on the sidewalk and doesn't even apologize when he nearly runs you over. He is the type of boy who when he's older drives his car fast and furiously. His friends all manifest similar traits; there's not one of them who seems to derive pleasure from any subject at school or achievement of any type. With his friends, he talks in a secret language that mixes profanities with slang. With adults, he talks in monosyllables.

Does this sound like your son? It may not sound like him at first, especially if you haven't been paying attention. However, if you are more observant and this picture fits him, then it is time to do something about it. Unfortunately, many men do nothing even when they realize that their boys are struggling. Sometimes they rationalize away their sons' behaviors. Other times they just get tired of dealing with teenage angst and rebellion. If you are working on your second, third, or fourth son, you may have had it up to here with all the arguments and problems. I know more than one father of multiple sons who has said something to the effect of, "My oldest boy was a terror when he was a teen and look, now he's in law school and doing fine." It's true that with age and maturity, some of these lost, lonely boys turn around their lives and end up great. Other boys, however, just go deeper and deeper into their isolation and alienation, and they don't end up fine.

Therefore, if your son seems like he's troubled, talk to him. He may not listen or want to engage in the types of dialogues I suggested in

Chapter 8, but eventually he will. When he resists your attempts to talk, try to reach him in some other way. Giving him a hug now and then might not seem like much, but it sends the message that he's not alone, that someone else is thinking about him. Don't be put off by his orange hair, nose ring, oversized pants, or rap music. Underneath it all, he is the same boy you bounced on your knee, hiked with on family vacations, and took to the park. Secretly, he wants your advice and ear. Make a commitment to get to know him again, and let him get to know you.

The obstacle to making this effort is going to be his off-putting and obnoxious behaviors. You are going to tell yourself: It's not worth it; he doesn't care what I think; he's being a jerk. When you hear yourself thinking these things, remind yourself of the following truism:

An adolescent bears a striking similarity to a two-year-old boy.

In other words, just as you don't take a two-year-old's temper tantrums as indicative of who he really is and what he thinks about you, don't take all your teenager's words and deeds at face value. What every two-year-old wants is to be noticed and cared for, and these are the same goals of your adolescent. What he says—no matter how hurtful it might be—is not always what he means. Accept this truth, and you will find it easier to make the first move toward reinvolvement in his life. The next move is learning to deal effectively with the 14 types of troubling teenage behaviors.

Tackling the 14 Types

Before talking about the 14 types of troubling teenage behaviors, you need to understand why your child exhibits these behaviors. Understanding the why will make it easier for you to accept the positive aspects of seemingly negative actions.

Erik Erickson, the famous developmental psychologist and researcher, theorized that adolescence is one of the most crucial developmental stages because by the end of this period a young boy must gain a firm sense of identity and life direction. The endless search for an inner and outer identity is the main task that all boys struggle with in this stage.

The search for a purpose, ideology, occupation, and a sexual, social, and physical identity creates issues that are just part of this journey. During this process, he is going to be experimenting with different ideas, clothes, interests, and romantic partners.

As much as you might wish that your son could skip this identity search and go straight to adulthood, this would be a bad idea. In fact, some teenagers do skip this identity quest—in part because of fathers who foisted an identity on them—and then end up as 40-year-old men who go through monumental midlife crises; they end up searching for their identities at age 40 rather than at age 16. When this happens, they often destroy their marriages and careers in the process.

Therefore, as much as possible, you need to allow your son to explore and find his identity. Expect him to reject his family tradition as a starting point for creating his own identity. If you are a super-achiever father, this is going to be particularly painful. It is as if he is throwing all your success and your desire for him to achieve similar success in your face. Understand, though, that this is not a rejection of you but rather a necessary step that your son needs to take toward clarifying who he will be. In fact, rejecting you is a positive sign. It means that he feels that he can break away from you without losing your love or support.

This does not mean that you give him carte blanche to reject and rebel against anything he doesn't like. Your role is to set boundaries for this rejection. You must establish limits on the degree to which he can experiment with his hairstyle, hair color, aggressive attitude, drugs, sexuality, friends, career choices, ideas, and relationships. In this way, he will be able to piece together his identity. I don't want to make this identity search sound simpler or easier than it actually is. Every day you will feel the tension as your son struggles with wanting your support and wanting nothing to do with you. You are going to find it confusing as he experiments with things you don't approve of and changes his mind countless times about what he wants, which brings us to the first of the 14 behaviors. I will describe each behavior briefly and then offer you some tips on how to deal with it.

Change

Your teenage son will change his mind about colleges, careers, clothes, girls, friends, and food. One day he may be a fast-food junkie and the next a vegetarian. No doubt he will appear to be fickle and contradictory. One day he will criticize you for being bourgeois, and almost in the same breath he will ask for thousands of dollars so that he can go on a class trip to Europe.

Tip: Don't try to reason with him; this isn't reasonable behavior. Try to see how he needs to view the world from a different angle and how it takes courage to try on and shed different identities. Your best stance is to be quiet. Accept each change as it comes, support him in his exploration, and don't criticize or make fun of him. Your only intervention should be if he's not changing. If he's not experimenting now, he may start when he's 40. Encourage him to try new things. Challenge him to take some reasonable risks. Dads can give their kids nudges and that can help them to gain the courage necessary to leave their childhood identity behind.

Identity Confusion

This is where your son tries out different personas and wonders which one fits. As he is experimenting and changes, he finds that he doesn't know if he's gay or straight, if he likes cheerleaders or punks, if he should be a doctor or a farmer. His expectations will rise when he is sure that he has found what he was meant to be, and then when he realizes that he is wrong, he will be crushed.

Tip: Treat each identity equally. It will only confuse him more if you add your two cents; he will be tempted to reject or accept the identity because you have voiced your opinion. Instead, show interest in his choices, ask questions about them, and be helpful if he needs information. However, don't try to influence him in any way.

Mood Swings

Your son's body during adolescence is flooded with as many hormones as a pregnant woman. These hormonal bursts make him feel like he is losing his mind and make you feel the same way as he switches from being happy to being irritable in a split second.

Tip: You can't talk him out of his moods, as much as you might want to try. Instead, grit your teeth and wait the mood out. Like the weather in Chicago, if you don't like it today, don't worry because it's bound to change tomorrow.

Aggression

Testosterone has been proven scientifically to be a hormone of aggression. Your son has more testosterone in his body than he knows what to do with or can handle. Part of forming a male identity is the ability to express his feelings. Frequently, aggression is the only acceptable emotion available for teenage boys who need to vent. For this reason, your son may love playing football and allowing his aggression to work for him on the field. On the other hand, if he is constantly getting in fights or verbally eviscerating others, this is unacceptable aggression.

Tip: Make sure that his aggression does not violate the behavioral limits you have set up. If it does, you have to intervene and follow through on the consequences for these violations. In addition, overly aggressive behavior can be a sign that your son has an underdeveloped identity. He is substituting aggression for exploring who he really is. If he doesn't stop being overly aggressive, you need to bring in a therapist.

Anger

Anger sometimes goes hand in hand with aggression, but it also can be a separate type of behavior. In other words, he doesn't "do" anything mean or harmful to others, but he becomes furious with himself, you, or others. It is natural for him to become angry, but it is not natural for him to be unable to control his anger. He needs to learn how to cope with his angry feelings. A civilized son becomes angry but does not let this anger disturb how he functions or allow it to destroy a relationship.

Tip: Talk to him about why he becomes angry. Explore the source of his anger and his trigger points. Perhaps he usually becomes angry when he receives a bad grade or when he has a disagreement with a friend. His anger may have deeper sources than you are capable of dealing with—it could go back to a childhood trauma, a divorce, or another problem when he was a boy—but giving him the opportunity to talk about his anger may help him to control it.

Approval-Seeking Behaviors

Many boys feel that they must strive to get their fathers' attention at any cost, and this need can intensify during adolescence. Frequently, the means of getting attention are self-defeating (e.g., school suspension, drug arrest, or poor grades).

Tip: Take these negative approval-seeking behaviors as a sign that your son feels neglected by you. He wants your love and attention, and if you don't give it to him, he will continue getting into trouble. Therefore, don't let a day go by without spending some time with him, talking and listening. If there's an activity you can convince him to do with you, do it. He will be less inclined to cause trouble if he can connect with you in a more positive manner.

Hyperactivity

While your son may have manifested this trait earlier in his life, teenage boys can exhibit it in spades. Attention deficit disorder (ADD) has been the subject of a lot of controversy—some people feel that boys are overdiagnosed with this disorder—but it is a very real problem and can drive dads to distraction. The common symptoms of ADD are inability to focus on discussions, poor organizational skills, short-term memory problems, difficulty concentrating on homework, poor processing of verbal information and directions, and being highly distractible. Boys are five times more likely than girls to have this disorder, and when they are adolescents, it can cause shame, guilt, and low self-esteem.

Tip: Not every hyperactive or ADD boy needs to receive Ritalin or other drugs, but for teenagers who are severely afflicted, drug treatment can mean a huge difference in their lives. You should at least get your son tested by a psychologist if he seems to have the aforementioned symptoms. If it's a mild case, you may want to channel his energy more productively. Sports are a great outlet, as are other activities involving physical movement, such as labor-intensive jobs, sculpture and painting, and dance and drama.

Hatred

In adolescence this intense feeling often involves a deep-seated emotional need to fit in with a group and the fear of not doing it. It is easier to hate a certain group (e.g., jocks, preps, surfers, geeks, or Christians) than to accept the perceived differences. The expression of hatred is an emotional defense for the wounds and pain caused by rejection—or even by the anticipation of rejection.

Tip: Because it is quite possible that your son's hatred will manifest itself as a mood rather than have a specific target, you may be confused about how to deal with it. What you'll see is your son being in a foul mood and hating everything from the asparagus you serve for dinner to his baby sister. Try to encourage him to dig beneath the surface of this mood to find the real object of his anger. This is going to be tough—his foul mood will make you want to run from him rather than talk to him—but the only way to dissipate the anger is by getting at the root of it. As you talk to him, be alert for someone or some group that has rejected him. Typically, it is the popular crowd or a particular clique of kids. Allowing him to talk about the specifics of the rejection or his fear of it happening will ratchet down his anger and make it more manageable. If your son's expressions of hatred are excessive and frequent, you may want to bring in professional help. It may require a trained therapist to help him dig beneath the surface and deal with the underlying emotion.

Love

The feelings of having a "crush" and walking 30 feet off the ground are typical, as is the ephemeral quality of these feelings. As superficial and as temporary as you suspect his "love" is, his intense feelings serve a purpose in his development. Falling in love helps to shape a teenage boy, giving him the chance to learn to respect women and also allowing him an opportunity to express his feelings. Being in love has a civilizing effect on most boys, preparing them for more mature relationships later on in life. It is better that he should make his mistakes now so that he will be more perceptive in the future about who he wants to be with.

Tip: Accept your son's feelings as genuine, even though you may think that the girl he has chosen is completely wrong for him and that he will grow tired of her in a matter of weeks. Give him every opportunity to express his feelings about his girlfriend. If possible, get to know the girl; she is a great source of information about your son and can help rather than hurt your relationship with him. During their romance, this girl has more influence over your son than anyone else in the world, so don't do anything that causes her to be a negative influence. Above all else, stop yourself from mocking his feelings or trying to talk him out of them. These are probably the fiercest emotions he has ever had, and if you dismiss them, he will turn that fierceness on you.

Male Friendships

At this age, male friends are as important to your son as sleep and food. They are his everyday emotional backboard and peer-group base. While his love interests may come and go, these friends are a steadying influence on his life. This core group supports him in ways that no one else can.

Tip: Get to know these guys and their parents, if possible. When your son talks to you, these boys' names will come up. They are the ones he is going to be spending the most time with, and if you know about them, you will be much better able to engage in good conversations with your son. Your awareness of these guys also will give you a sense of your son's developing interests and potential for trouble. Figure out if his friends are good or bad students, athletes, or slackers. Do they spend a lot of time in the library or hanging around on street corners? Are they a "fast" crowd, or are they the dweebs and geeks?

Drug and Alcohol Use

To a certain extent, experimentation with certain drugs such as marijuana is to be expected. Chronic use is where kids get into real trouble. Frequently, chronic use is a form of self-medication for depression, anxiety, self-esteem issues, or other interpersonal problems. Chronic drug use is a detriment to your son's emotional development. Addicts are usually emotionally arrested at the age of 15 and stop developing beyond the teenage stage of invincibility. The same holds true for chronic drinking; it raises the same red flags as chronic drug use.

Tip: In the last chapter I stressed that dads should not romanticize their own youthful drug or alcohol use. Similarly, you should not excuse your son's usage just because you did the same thing when you were a teenager. It may be that you smoked marijuana a few times during high school, but your son may be smoking dope a few times every week. While some experimentation with "soft" drugs and liquor should be expected, chronic use means that you need to intervene. Intervention can mean getting your son into therapy to getting him into special treatment programs. Because kids are clever at disguising their use from parents, you are going to have to snoop around a bit if you think he has a serious problem. This means talking to his friends and the parents of his friends, his teachers, and others who observe him daily. Watch how he spends his money. If he is always broke yet makes money at a job, be aware that the object of his spending might be drugs.

Commitments

Teenage boys often make commitments to things beyond their school classes, such as jobs or sports teams or music. These are real-world activities that provide your son with a forum to test himself and his abilities. Commitments serve as an identity-building process, giving boys a sense of how hard work and dedication yield satisfaction and other rewards.

Tip: Insist that your son honor his commitments. Frequently, dads allow their sons to weasel out of commitments because they feel sorry for them. When a son says he wants to quit the baseball team because practice takes too much time, the dad often says fine. When a son decides that his summer job is boring, dad empathizes and tells him he can quit and find another one. Allowing this type of quitting is sending the wrong message. Boys need to learn that not everything in life is fun or easy and that sticking it out—at least for a reasonable period of time—can be a means to an end. Teenagers are notoriously impulsive, and this impulsivity can get them in trouble. Insisting that your son honor his commitments teaches him the value of stick-to-itiveness. Obviously, there are exceptions to this rule. If your son seems to be on the verge of a nervous breakdown because of a sadistic coach, he may have good reason to break his commitment. It's also possible that you have an overachieving son who has taken on too much, and he simply doesn't have the ability to do everything he's signed up for. If it is necessary for him to break a commitment, though, he needs a good reason. Don't allow him to get out of something just because he doesn't feel like doing it.

Physical Appearance (Body Image)

Boys, much like girls, feel pressure to look like pro athletes, models, or music and movie stars. For this reason, they will adopt certain hair and clothing styles that you may find offensive. Your son also will be extremely self-critical of how he looks and sensitive to criticism of any aspect of his appearance. Unfortunately, boys are terribly cruel to each other at this age and seize on any flaw—acne, weight gain, or lack of the "right" clothes—and use it to make fun of other boys.

Tip: Assume that your son will be highly sensitive to anything you say about his appearance. Therefore, don't criticize or offer insincere compliments. Instead, focus on his strengths as a person. Praise his specific acts of generosity, intelligence, or compassion or any other act that represents his inner substance. He is still going to be obsessed to some extent with his appearance, but you are reminding him that there's more to a person than how he or she looks. Sooner or later, he will get it.

Cheap Thrills

Teenage boys love speed and excitement, whether it's a real or virtual experience. They relish fast cars, skateboard parks, violent video games and movies, loud music, and lamebrained stunts. These behaviors are all designed to give your son a sense of feeling alive and powerful. They create a buzz that helps him escape from his humdrum existence and allows him to feel courageous and even triumphant. Listening to loud music—especially music that is profane and provocative—gives them a sense of identity, even if it is ultimately a hollow one. It's their music, after all, not yours, and that's what counts.

Tip: Most of these behaviors are harmless, the exception being driving fast. Set limits on the driving, and enforce them: If your son receives a speeding ticket or commits any sort of driving violation, he should receive a significant punishment. With the other cheap thrills, allow him these experiences, even if you find the music he listens to or the video games he plays repulsive. You can learn a lot about your son by paying attention to the particular thrills he gravitates toward. Maybe he plays that one video game night and day because he feels bullied and demeaned by the other kids, and the game allows him to be a hero.

Whatever the message is, recognize it and use it to help communicate with him.

Recognize and respond to these 14 types of teenage behaviors, and you will find that both you and your son will tolerate them better. You will be able to provide some good advice and a receptive ear for your son when he is involved in these behaviors, and he will be less likely to take these behaviors to extremes.

The extreme is what every father worries about because it means that their child is in real trouble. Let's look at the real dangers facing teenagers and how you can spot the red flags and take action to coax your child away from the edge.

10

The Great Depression

Help Your Son Overcome the Darkness of Adolescence

O N THE SURFACE, your teenager may not seem to be any more depressed than other boys his age. Sure, he may mope around the house at times or sit staring out the window with a sad look on his face, but you tell yourself that he is fine and that he will snap out of it. Maybe he will. Be aware, however, that you may be unable or unwilling to deal with your son's dark moods. Men reflexively minimize the seriousness of male adolescent depression because they don't want to admit that their sons aren't happy. They aren't accustomed to thinking or talking about this subject; they don't know how to communicate with their sons about what they are feeling. It's scary for dads to realize that their sons are sad, lacking hope, or depressed. Typically, this scariness translates into a counterproductive response. More often than not, dads try to rouse their sons out of these dark moods by making a joke of the situation or shaming their sons by saying, "There are a lot of boys who are a lot worse off than you." They also may yell at their depressed sons, hoping to "jar" them out of their blue mood.

Think about how you would react to the following situation:

You come home from work and see your son staring listlessly at the television or lying on the couch gazing vacantly at the ceiling; this has been going on for a week. He has barely communicated with you or your wife beyond a few grunted responses. You have asked him what's wrong, assuming that something negative happened at school, but he insists it's "nothing."

Would you

A. Feel like whatever it is that's ailing him doesn't seem serious and that you'll do more harm than good if you try and force him to talk about it.
B. Overcome your discomfort and keep trying to talk to him about the cause of his listlessness, and if he doesn't respond, insist that he see a therapist.

Most dads would choose option A. This is a bad choice for a number of reasons. At worst, your son may be clinically depressed, and a suicide attempt is a possibility. At best, his down mood could have serious future consequences. It could negatively affect his friendships and his grades, it could cause him to drop out of school or refuse to go to college, and it could become a pattern in his life, one in which he takes comfort in sadness and the listless, hopeless feelings that accompany it whenever things don't work out as he hoped they would.

As a father, you need to help your son learn to cope with life's downs as well as its ups. By recognizing the underlying causes and ramifications of his moodiness, you'll be in a good position to help him cope.

Male Depression

A boy's depression is different from a girl's depression. The normal clinical scales of measuring depression are based on the symptoms most associated with teenage girls and women. As a result, depression is hard to diagnose in boys because the very common behaviors associated with this state—crying, anorexia, dependence on others and then rejecting their help—may not be present. Many boys who are depressed are misdiagnosed as being oppositional, socially withdrawn, or just going through a normal adolescent phase. In fact, they may not even fit the criteria of my earlier example. They may be doing okay at school and may be involved in social activities. As boys, they have been conditioned to hide their emotions, so their symptoms may be more subtle than you would expect.

Male depression, however, can be deadly. Suicide attempts are a by-product of this depressed state. Even if it doesn't have this terrible consequence, though, depression can dramatically and negatively affect a boy's life. The sooner depression is spotted, the better it can be treated. Dads more than anyone else are in the best position to identify the problem and intervene. They don't do so, though, because they are not prepared to admit that their sons are depressed and they are not aware of the signs of male depression. They don't realize that displays of aggression, anger, hatred, self-defeating gestures, rebellious actions, and drug use all may mask an underlying sadness or deeper depression.

I'm not trying to be an alarmist when I warn that untreated depression in teenaged boys can lead to suicide attempts. It is simply that I have worked with too many parents whose boys have attempted to kill themselves. Even if these attempts result only in superficial injury, they represent desperate cries for help that previously were going unheard. You don't want to have a boy who even entertains suicidal thoughts. Although he may never act on these thoughts, he still will be suffering emotionally, and his development may be retarded.

The time for you to act is when he is on the cusp of mild depression or before—*not* when he is in the throes of it. To act, you need to move past your anger at his spiked hair and outrageous behavior and see beneath it to the little boy asking for help. Many times fathers get so mad at their sons for these outrageous behaviors that they punish them and miss the hidden message of despair and hopelessness. This emotional miscommunication between father and son escalates the negative cycle of behavior and can lead to depression and suicide attempts.

Carl is the 40-year-old dad of three sons. The oldest, Rick, is 15, and to all outward appearances, nothing seemed to be amiss. As a freshman in high school, Rick was receiving decent grades, although Carl knew he should be doing better based on his high aptitude tests. Although Rick wasn't participating in any extracurricular activities, he was interested in art, sometimes drawing cartoons in his room after school; he talked about taking art classes over the summer. Rick found a new group of friends at the start of high school, and although Carl didn't particularly approve of them—they were somewhat unsavory looking and didn't care much about school or grades—he figured that Rick probably would have a new set of friends by his sophomore year.

As his freshman year progressed, Rick became increasingly outrageous in his behaviors and appearance. He colored his hair green and wore a nose ring, he began ditching school, he and his friends were caught drinking in the park after curfew, and he became increasingly snappish and boorish in his behavior toward his younger brothers.

Every morning, Carl woke Rick for school because he was having trouble rising when his alarm rang. One morning a few weeks before the end of the school year, Carl shook Rick, but he didn't open his eyes. Carl quickly saw the half-empty bottle of aspirin on the nightstand and a note addressed to him and his wife. Later, after the ambulance had taken Rick to the emergency room and they'd pumped his stomach, Carl read the note. It was a rambling, highly theatrical suicide note. In it Rick admitted to being "blue" and spent a lot of the note "willing" his record collection and clothes to various friends. In one sense, the suicide attempt wasn't serious—he hadn't taken enough aspirin to do much harm. In another sense, though, it was deadly serious. There was a line in the suicide note where Rick asked his dad to "pay more attention to Tom and Josh [his younger brothers] than you paid to me."

Carl hadn't seen any of this coming. Your son may not make a suicide attempt, but he may harbor the same feelings of hopelessness and sadness that caused Rick to do what he did. To prevent this from happening, you need to be alert to the traits of teenage male depression.

The Unlucky 13 Traits

The following list of 13 symptoms may vary from boy to boy, but they are very typical of teenage male depression. Your son may have a few of these symptoms and be depressed. He doesn't need to manifest all or a majority of them to be in the danger zone. It is the severity of each symptom and its level of disturbance in your son's daily functioning that need to be evaluated. When describing each of the following traits, I will provide you with some tips and techniques for evaluating your son's specific symptoms.

1. *School performance declines.* Your son's grades drop suddenly, he doesn't turn in homework assignments, and he loses enthusiasm

and interest in school. He may have been an excellent student who becomes merely a good one, a good one who becomes average, or an average one who becomes poor. There is at least one level drop in his performance, and neither you nor he can explain it. If depression is the cause, he is simply too unhappy to focus on his schoolwork and get it done. If he is smart, he may be able to get by without flunking every class, but his attitude will change. He won't be excited even about his favorite class, and he'll be indifferent to whatever grades he receives.

HOW TO EVALUATE

Just about every boy exhibits a decline in grades at some point, so don't jump to conclusions just because his grades are worse for one quarter or he doesn't do some homework assignments. To determine if this decline represents a more serious condition, do the following:

- *See how long his school performance decline lasts.* If it's more than a school quarter—if it lasts a semester or longer—then this might be a sign that he is depressed.
- *Investigate whether there is a specific cause for the decline.* It may be that your son is overwhelmed with extracurricular activities, has taken a part-time job, or has a particularly heavy course load this year. Or he may simply be taking more difficult classes. If you can pinpoint a cause, then it is less likely that he is depressed.
- *Assess whether his attitude has changed along with his grades.* Observe him, and ask his teachers for their observations. Does he seem less interested in his favorite class? Is he falling asleep in class, whereas before he never did? Does he respond to your questions about school with even less enthusiasm than he normally shows? Does he show complete indifference to falling grades or negative feedback about him you receive from his teachers?

    2. *Sudden change in behavior.* Your son becomes impulsive or appears very depleted physically and emotionally. He might appear listless, enervated, dispassionate, bored and sluggish; normal activities are no longer of any interest or concern to

him. His behavioral change might also be in the other direction. Suddenly, he becomes energized; it seems like he's always in motion, bouncing from one activity to the next. While he once could sit for hours with a book he enjoyed or spend a long amount of time doing puzzles or playing board games, now he can't sit still for more than a few minutes.

How to Evaluate

Adolescence is a time of behavioral change, but be on the lookout for sudden, radical change, especially at both ends of the activity spectrum. If your son suddenly becomes listless or manically energized, this may be a sign of depression. Here are two other ways to evaluate these behaviors:

- *If your son is highly energized, watch for impulsive, unpredictable, or irrational behavior.* These three traits can indicate a more serious problem than just typical teenage hyperactivity.
- *If your son is listless, determine if there's a reason for his exhaustion.* Teenage boys often burn the candle at both ends, and he simply may be burned out. Is he getting enough sleep at night? Is he involved in a sport that is making significant demands on his time and energy?

  3. *Sudden interest in drugs and alcohol.* The use of emotionally deadening drugs is a classic hallmark of depression in teenage boys as well as adults. The drug of choice tends to be marijuana, which acts like a sedative for uncomfortable feelings. As I noted earlier, many teenagers experiment with drugs and alcohol, and this experimentation is not a sign of depression. It is when the experimentation turns into a habit or pattern that it may be a sign that your son is struggling.

How to Evaluate

To assess whether your son's interest in drugs and alcohol has gone beyond the experimental stage, look at the following three factors:

- *Frequency.* Is he using drugs or alcohol three or more times weekly?
- *Degree of intoxication.* Does he seem perpetually stoned? Is he "out of it" for significant amounts of time? Is it difficult for him

to communicate clearly? All this suggests that he is using drugs or alcohol to self-medicate his depression rather than just for kicks.

- *Use of drugs or alcohol with others.* Boys who experiment with drugs and alcohol usually do it in groups. Boys who self-medicate usually do it alone.

4. *Legal problems (i.e., he is arrested) and authority problems.* Your son has no regard for school or home rules, laws, or preset limits/boundaries. He is insisting on complete autonomy. His favorite responses to your limits are "Leave me alone," "Get away from me," and "It's my life; no one can control me." Boys who get in trouble with the law tend to be depressed and are "acting out" their feelings on others or any structure (rules) that is close to them.

HOW TO EVALUATE

Many boys get at least one speeding ticket or are caught out after curfew on occasion. These isolated incidents aren't indicators of the depression. Instead, use the following as an evaluation guide:

- *Determine if your son loses respect for authority suddenly.* Some kids are chronic troublemakers. Others suddenly seem to change, and members of this latter group are more likely to be depressed.
- *Watch for "rebels without a cause."* In other words, if your son seems to be challenging all authority for no particular reason (such as protesting against an unfair teacher), then he may be depressed.

5. *Overinvolvement in sports, school, and work.* Working hard at school, sports, or a job is always positive, but some boys may use these activities to distract themselves from their depressed frame of mind; it is similar to how adult workaholics distract themselves from personal problems. Boys don't want to confront their sadness and aloneness, and this overinvolvement allows them a momentary respite from their feelings.

HOW TO EVALUATE

This is a tricky one, in that you are looking for negatives in a positive. Still, you know your son, and you probably can sense if he is throwing himself into an activity beyond his normal level of interest. To ascertain if this is the case, ask him the following question:

- Why are you working so hard at _____?

If he tells you how much he loves it and that it really matters to him, this is a good response. If he can't give you an answer or gives you a superficial one, such as, "Because that's what the coach or teacher expects," be aware that this may be a sign of depression.

6. *Odd response to a significant relationship loss.* Boys view emotional attachment as a weakness rather than as a sign of emotional maturity. Many times they react to a significant relationship loss with stoicism rather than with outward sadness or disappointment. When they can't express their emotions, they are vulnerable to depression. When they are devastated by or furious about a break up and can't talk about how sad it makes them feel, they may head straight toward depression.

HOW TO EVALUATE

This is a relatively simple one. If you know that your son has just experienced a significant relationship loss and outwardly displays no feelings about it, you can assume that depression is a possibility.

7. *Sleeps excessively, has loss of appetite, or shows weight gain.* These types of physical symptoms are considered the vegetative signs of depression. Any problems with sustained concentration, sleeping, eating, anorexia, bulimia, obesity, headaches, and stomachaches are also possible signs.

HOW TO EVALUATE

Of course, teenage boys sleep excessively because their bodies are starved for sleep, they don't eat because they are too busy running from one activity to the next, and they can gain weight from eating too much junk food and too few decent meals. Therefore, try to apply common sense to your evaluation of these behaviors. There is a difference between a few sleeping binges every few weeks to make up for lost sleep and consistently going to bed at eight in the evening and still having trouble getting up the next morning. If your son refuses his favorite foods or devours everything in sight like a starving man—and does this day after day—then he may be exhibiting classic signs of depression.

8. *Social withdrawal and loss of longtime friends.* This is an unambiguous sign that something is wrong. When teenage boys are depressed, they withdraw from people and isolate themselves from their close friends. Close friendships require emotional involvement, and depressed boys don't have the energy or interest to sustain these relationships. Your son suddenly may be involved with a new group of friends, and if he is depressed, he has made this choice because this new group lacks knowledge of who he was before to challenge him about his new behaviors and attitudes.

How to Evaluate

Talk to his old group of friends, and ask them if they challenged your son about how he was acting. Did they find that he was acting strangely? Did he become defensive about his new behaviors when they questioned him? Did he drift away from their group shortly after that?

9. *Appearance change (e.g., poor hygiene, wears same shirt daily).* If your son looks unwashed, unshaven, and smells awful, these aren't typical teenage male behaviors. Although teenagers can be slovenly and dress inappropriately, looking and smelling like a homeless person can be a warning sign of depression. When male teens exhibit this behavior, often they are unaware of the decline in their appearance because they are so distracted by their feelings of isolation and hopelessness.

How to Evaluate

At times, it is tough for parents to differentiate between a messy son and an unhygienic one. At first glance the boy who is wearing pants four sizes too big for him and has spiked green hair and unlaced sneakers may not seem much different from a boy who hasn't taken a shower for three days. There is, however, a difference, and the following may help you to make this distinction:

- *Assess whether he is aware of how he looks and smells.* If he is conscious of his appearance—if he is appearing this way to make some sort of statement—then it is not indicative of a depressed state. If he is truly unaware, this means that he is distracted by his inner conflicts and turmoil.

- *Think about whether he also seems disinterested and distracted.* A "flat affect" goes hand in hand with this type of appearance. Both his demeanor and his personal hygiene reflect his inability to pull himself together and act age-appropriately.

10. *Poor concentration and loss of interest in hobbies and life.* Loss of the ability to focus, inability to finish tasks or follow through on assignments, and inability to remember simple things are all depression-related traits.

HOW TO EVALUATE

Your son may not notice any of these traits, and if you start questioning him about them, he may honestly not know what you are talking about. A better way to evaluate this symptom is to look at whether he has simply dropped passions in his life. Did he used to love rock and roll music and now barely listens to it? If he has replaced one passion with another one, this is great and suggests that this isn't a sign of depression. If he has just given up his interests and has failed to replace them, then it may well signal that he is in trouble. If he also can't concentrate on any activity for more than a few minutes, then take it as added proof that he is mired in feelings of hopelessness.

11. *Discusses the purposelessness of life.* You may have expressed these same sentiments in college or as a young man, but when middle-school or high-school boys talk this way, it is more than an intellectual conceit. Although some boys will say nothing about how alone and despairing they feel, others will talk about almost nothing else. This may be a sign that a boy's depression is severe and that he needs immediate help.

HOW TO EVALUATE

The following two factors should be assessed:

- *The length of time that he talks about life's lack of meaning.* In other words, does he talk about it all the time over a period of days, or is it something he mentions infrequently and usually in relationship to a specific event (e.g., the death of a friend or relative)? If he talks about it virtually nonstop for five days or more, then he is asking for help, and you need to get it for him.

- *References to suicide.* This should be an obvious red flag, but I have known dads of boys who attempted suicide who dismissed their sons' references to killing themselves. They said that they thought their sons were just being melodramatic and didn't mean to be taken literally. Suicide references combined with talk of suicide can be a deadly combination. Get your son help immediately.

12. *Violence.* The most common manifestation is a fistfight with a peer, but it also may take the form of violence toward strangers, family, animals, and himself. This is the external expression of the rage and unhappiness that are part of every boy's depression. A deeper need isn't being addressed—a need for love and belonging—and until it is, a boy may strike out in frustration.

HOW TO EVALUATE

While teenage boys may get in fistfights every so often, such fights usually happen only once in a great while. It is frequent fighting and other forms of violence for which you need to be vigilant. Specifically:

- *Watch for escalating levels and frequency of violence.* This escalation indicates depression. Getting in a greater number of fights and ones where another boy suffers more serious injury are signs of desperation.

13. *Rejects family, avoids assistance, and denies pain.* When a teenage boy will not accept help from you, it may signal depression. Depressed boys reflexively shut down their perceptions of their feelings, trying to numb themselves to their unhappiness. They want to disengage from their depression, but this is a bad coping technique in that all they end up doing is pushing it deeper down inside of them. Sooner or later it resurfaces, more powerful than it was before.

HOW TO EVALUATE

Examine how your son reacts to an offer of help. If his reaction is extreme—if he becomes angry or highly demonstrative in his rejection—this may indicate that he is fighting not to acknowledge his sadness.

Intervention: What to Do If You Think Your Son Is Headed for Trouble

Better than anyone else, you know if your son is exhibiting the signs of a depressed adolescent. Better than anyone else, you are in a position to do something about it. Too many fathers cede intervention responsibility to their wives, and this is often a mistake. While women are often very perceptive about their sons and good at setting limits, they are not male authority figures. If a boy is depressed, he needs the most important male authority figure in his life to help him.

You possess tremendous power, and you need to use this power to help your son as soon as he exhibits the symptoms just described. Ideally, you have been an involved and aware father all along, and this involvement and awareness often help boys to avoid falling into depression during their teenage years. Even if it doesn't, your active participation in your son's life will provide you with unique insight about your son, and you should be able to spot the symptoms I have discussed before anyone else.

Once you see symptoms emerge, follow this seven-step program that will help you to gather additional information about your son's condition and take appropriate action to help him get through this difficult period in his life:

1. Confirm Your Perceptions

You may have done some confirmation as a result of the evaluation tips provided previously, but you should make every effort to follow up with other sources to ascertain if your son is depressed. It may be that he is in a predepressed state, exhibiting very mild signs of this condition. Or it is possible that you have completely misread his behaviors. I know of one father who was convinced that his son was depressed because he suddenly started eating very little and seemed very anxious and decided not to go out for the basketball team, a sport that he had once loved. It turned out that the son had decided to go out for the wrestling team, was dieting in order to make a weight class, and was anxious about whether he could do it.

Talk to the people who regularly interact with your son about the symptoms you believe you have observed. These people may include friends, your other children, your wife, coaches, teachers, counselors, and anyone else who seems relevant. You don't have to grill these people or even let on that you suspect that your son is depressed. A question such as, "Have you noticed anything different about _____ lately?" is often all that is needed.

2. *Assess the Severity of His Condition*

While you haven't been trained to make a clinical diagnosis, you probably can make a good guess about the shape your son is in. To make this assessment, figure out where your son stands regarding the following two factors:

- How many of the 13 symptoms apply to him.
- What is the intensity of each symptom on a scale of 1 to 5, with 5 being the most severe.

In terms of the second factor, the most severe rating means that your son is exhibiting a given behavior consistently in its most extreme form. For instance, he has lost all his close friends and spends almost every waking moment that he is not in school by himself in his room with the door shut. If he has only lost half his friends and is only in his room with the door shut two nights each week, he might receive a 3 rating rather than the previous 5.

Obviously, this is not a scientific method, and your fears for your son can unconsciously inflate a 1 into a 5. You may jump to conclusions based on one incident or because you were a depressed boy and are convinced your son is spiraling into the same dark cycle. Therefore, "double-check" your intensity rating. Some people find it beneficial to write a rationale for a rating, using the writing process as a way to explore whether their feelings are getting in the way of their objectivity. When you put your rationale into writing, you often can gain clarity that is lacking when you keep thoughts locked in your head. You can spot hyperbole and inaccuracies better when you read them than when you think about them.

This severity rating is important because it tells you how quickly you need to intervene. If your son is a 5, you need to do something immediately. The possibility of suicide is always there, and even if this seems highly unlikely, you don't want to take a chance. If you only give your son a 1 or 2, it is possible that he is not depressed, and you can observe his behavior for a while before doing anything. Still, be careful of "cheating" on your rating in order to reassure yourself that everything is okay, which brings us to the next step.

3. Fight Your Denial Reflex

It is doubly difficult for fathers to admit that their sons are in emotional trouble. As a man, you don't like to admit emotional weakness. As a father, you don't like to think that your son has this problem—it is a bad reflection on you. As a result, you are going to be tempted to deny that anything serious is wrong.

Force yourself to move past this denial. Remind yourself that your son is a separate being from you—that his reactions to life are his own and not yours. Being depressed is not a crime or a weakness, and it does not have to affect his life negatively. As you deal with your denial reflex, do not accept his condition but move from denial into anger and frustration. You are not going to do your son any good if you angrily confront him about his symptoms and demand that he change. Disciplining him for being depressed is absurd; threatening him is a waste of time. This is not a matter of willpower. You will push him deeper into his depression if you give him ultimatums. Whether his depression is chemical, a result of complex factors from his past, or a combination of the two, he simply cannot snap out of it. He needs your empathy and support, not your anger. Accept that he is depressed—or that he is heading toward this state—and resolve to help see him through it.

4. Bring in a Therapist

This is not an admission of your failure as a father. To the contrary, it is testimony to your success. If you bring in a therapist, you are demonstrating your willingness to do anything necessary to help your son. Therapy can be a place where your son learns to express his feelings without being shamed or questioned. Someone trained in recognizing and treating male depression can be invaluable in helping your son to overcome it because he or she knows the dark, foreboding mindscape your son inhabits. I've mentioned a number of extreme instances when therapeutic intervention is warranted, especially when a boy's behaviors are suicidal or violent. Therapy, however, can be highly beneficial for mood disorders such as depression. I have seen many depressed teenagers emerge from this state relatively quickly because they had the help of a therapist. I am not going to argue here for a specific type of therapist— social worker, psychologist, or psychiatrist—but I would suggest finding someone who has experience working with adolescents. Your son's school will have a list of therapists it recommends.

5. Consider Medication

Your son's depression may be biologically based, and if this is the case, medication can be helpful. Do not automatically reject medication or discourage your son from thinking about this option. Research shows that the human body needs a chemical homeostasis in the brain. An imbalance results from a shortage of certain neurotransmitters (chemicals in the brain). One such chemical is called *serotonin,* and it directly affects emotional well-being. Medications called *selective serotonin reuptake inhibitors* (SSRIs) are available to correct this imbalance. Some of the current prescription medications include Prozac (fluoxetine), Zoloft (sertraline), and Paxil (paroxetine).

At the same time, recognize that medication is not the complete answer to your son's depression. Research shows that the balance of neurotransmitters is also affected by psychological events, such as daily stress, loss of a loved one, or a severe early-life trauma (e.g., death of a parent). All these events can change the biological and chemical workings of the brain and leave an individual vulnerable to depression. Therefore, drugs aren't a panacea for what ails your son. You still need to be a conscious, involved father, especially if you have a son who is depressed.

6. Call the Police or Institutionalize Your Son If You Suspect That He Is Suicidal

This is a tough call in more ways than one, and you certainly do not want to take these drastic measures on scant evidence. If, however, you have gone through the preceding five steps, you should have a pretty good idea of your son's state of mind. It may well be that his suicidal tendencies have come up in discussions with his therapist or that his girlfriend told you that he threatened to kill himself after they broke up.

A sobering statistic is that although women attempt suicide more often than men, men are three times more successful at it than women. Sadly, boys often choose more effective methods to end their lives—guns, jumping from high buildings, and so on.

Ideally, you will intervene using the preceding steps and prevent your son from ever reaching this suicidal point. If these steps fail, however, you need to be prepared to do whatever it takes to stop your son from letting his depression push him over the edge.

7. Increase Your Awareness of, Involvement with, and Empathy Toward Your Son

This may be the last thing you want to do, especially if your son is manifesting symptoms such as violence, legal problems, and rejection of family. It seems like he doesn't want anything to do with you, and you may be so fed up with his behavior that you don't want anything to do with him. If it is any help, remember that underneath all that obnoxious behavior there is a boy who needs your help. It is also possible that you bear some responsibility for his current condition. I am not trying to make you feel guilty, and I am not saying that your son shouldn't be responsible for his own actions. One of the points I have emphasized throughout this book, however, is that fathers are often absent, neglectful, and rejecting of their sons, and this contributes to problems they experience both as boys and as adults. Before, you didn't realize how your parenting was affecting your son. Now you do. Therefore, use the knowledge you have gained to be a better father now than you were in the past.

Specifically, encourage your son to think and talk about his feelings of isolation and hopelessness. This will be tough at first because depressed boys often lack the maturity, verbal ability, or insight to express their dark, painful feelings. They also are constrained by a society that discourages men from expressing any dark feelings except anger. A boy's male heroes—professional athletes, movie stars, rock stars—rarely express sadness and remorse. Instead, they create tough-as-nails images, and boys attempt to follow suit.

Help your son to get past these fictional personas and get real. Although there is no foolproof method for encouraging your son to express his dark feelings, here are two things any dad can do:

- *Share your own feelings of sadness, dashed dreams, and regret with him.* Model the behavior you want him to adopt. He may mock or ignore your emotional expressions—especially if he is not used to hearing you talk about your dark feelings—but he also may respond in kind eventually.

- *Discover his deepest, darkest secret.* In reality, it is probably not particularly dark or deep, but it seems that way to him. It might be that he is ashamed of being "stupid" and feels that he is too dumb to ever be successful in life. It might be that he feels so awkward around girls that he is convinced he will never have a romantic relationship. Encouraging him to reveal this secret isn't as difficult as it might appear, but you need to be patient. Just be open and nonjudgmental in your discussions with him and give him opportunities to talk. He wants to let you know how he feels, but it has be on his terms and at his speed. He may let the secret out in dribs and drabs, alluding to it and circling around the subject. Don't minimize it by telling him, "That's nothing to be ashamed of." Just listen, ask questions, and let him feel ready to talk about it.

11

Meeting the Challenges of Being a Twenty-First-Century Dad

It seems like it was a lot easier to be a father years ago. We live in such a complex world. I mean, half the people I know are divorced, and sometimes there are two stepfathers involved in raising a kid. Plus, people's values are all out of whack, especially in the affluent community where I live. I'm trying my best to raise good boys, but the odds seemed like they're stacked against me.

Greg, 37, father of two young sons

IN CERTAIN WAYS, it is more difficult to be a father today, especially a father to boys. The challenges now seem far more formidable than years ago. Back then, boys had good role models. U.S. presidents such as Dwight David Eisenhower and Harry S Truman seemed to represent the best of us, and we could hope that our sons would grow up to be like them. Sports heroes such as Joe DiMaggio and Jim Thorpe represented rags-to-riches stories and offered lessons in perseverance. A comedian such as Bob Hope devoted a lot of his time to charitable works, and an actor such as Jimmy Stewart seemed as noble and self-effacing in real life as he was on the screen.

Today the people in role-model positions include former President Bill Clinton, sports heroes such as Allen Iversen and Pete Rose, and actors such as Robert Downey, Jr., and Nick Nolte.

Just as significantly, we have become a much more cynical society. In the past, our cultural and religious institutions inculcated ideals in our boys. From the Boy Scouts to the television show "Father Knows Best" to church sermons on Sunday, our society sent strong messages to boys about right and wrong. As corny as it sounds today, we believed in male gallantry, nobility, and self-sacrifice.

Now, irony and sarcasm dominate the messages kids receive. Many boys are heavily influenced by rap music, popular movies and television shows, and commercials. Because they are less likely to be religious or to join and stay with scouts, boys are vulnerable to the cynical tenor of the times we live in. Everyone from late-night talk show hosts to disk jockeys to singers takes on a hip, jaded persona. As a result, boys resist sincerity, generosity, and kindness because they are decidedly unhip.

Neighborhoods used to be places where boys learned good values, and if they got out of line, a neighbor—usually a male—would immediately put them in their place. The tight-knit nature of most communities meant that parents would know immediately if their son had done something wrong, and more likely than not, dad would punish him for his transgression. Now neighborhoods tend to be less tight-knit and more transient; it is quite possible that the next-door neighbors don't even know what your son looks like.

Finally, most parents aren't at home as much as they were in the past. This is due in part to the changing world of work; people simply have to work harder and longer in more competitive industries. In a global world, professional people not only must be on the "road" more, but that road also often stretches into countries on the other side of the earth from their homes. When both parents work, this deepens the moral vacuum. Kids are being raised by nannies and au pairs who may be unwilling or unable to communicate good values to children. While this hurts the moral development of both girls and boys, boys are especially vulnerable. Whether or not women work, they tend to invest more time and effort in parenting, modeling behaviors and values for their daughters. In addition, when both parents are working, a female authority figure—often a grandmother or another female relative— becomes the substitute caregiver, leaving boys without a consistent male presence.

All these trends and events make it imperative that men be more conscious and involved as fathers than in the past. To face these challenges effectively, you must make the effort to understand how your own father's parenting has affected your fathering style, and you also must be aware of the dos and don'ts as your son moves through his developmental stages.

The good news is that we know a lot more about being a father to a son than we did in the past. I have tried to share much of this knowledge with you throughout the book, but I would like to add three additional points here that will help you to meet the challenges you will face as a father in the coming years. Specifically, let's look at the following:

- How to interact with your wife to raise an emotionally healthy son.
- How to deal with divorce and stepparenting in ways that will help rather than hinder your son's development.
- How to instill a strong moral sense in your son in an increasingly amoral world.

Your Wife, His Mother: Finding the Proper Intersection of Roles

You are not in this parenting business alone, assuming that your wife is an involved parent. Even if you are divorced, she has a critical role to play in helping to raise your son. I haven't devoted much space to a woman's role in child raising because most women are good at taking on this role naturally. Unlike men, they usually recognize this as their responsibility and spend time with and invest emotional energy in their son's upbringing. They don't need to be told to "Mother your son."

At the same time, however, men need to understand that their wives are valuable resources they can call on as they struggle to redefine their own roles as fathers. Even if you are divorced from the mother of your son, you should still communicate regularly about your son and make decisions about him together. Your wife can provide you with valuable feedback both about your own fathering style and perhaps even that of your father as well as information about your son's state of mind and evolving behaviors. It is quite possible that she is more emotionally tuned in to him than you are, and even though she can't substitute for you as a male role model/authority figure, she can confirm your suspicions about what is going on beneath his surface behaviors.

Therefore, regularly talk with your wife about all the issues involved in your fathering experience. More specifically, have her help you with the following:

- *Ask her how, based on her observations, your father relates to you.* Does she perceive him as a time-bomb father, a passive type, or a compassionate mentor?
- *Talk with her about your strengths and weaknesses as a father.* Does she think that you spend enough time with your son? Are you able to express a range of emotions in his presence? Are you involved in his life in terms of both physical attendance and listening and responding to how he feels? Are you verbally or physically abusive? What are you doing that is helping your son to grow and develop in positive ways?
- *Talk with her about how you can share in more of the parenting responsibilities with your son.* If she is doing the lion's share of parenting, talk about what you can both do together and which jobs you can take over from her so that the responsibilities are equitably divided.
- *Request that she share her observations with you about your son's attitudes and actions during each developmental stage.* This is especially important during adolescence, when he may be too angry at you or intimidated by you to share his feelings. From what she tells you, you can start rebuilding emotional bridges to your son.

You also should recognize that how you act with and toward your wife will affect your son. From the time he is a little boy, he closely watches what you do and say when you are with his mother. More than this, he quickly picks up on how you feel about her, reading between the lines of even small gestures and expressions. You are modeling behaviors that will shape his attitude toward women as well as his feelings toward you. A special bond exists between mother and son, and if you are abusive toward her, it will affect your relationship with him. Treat her with respect and love, and it not only will give him a wonderful model to use in how he relates to the women in his life, but it also will strengthen your relationship with him.

Boys also benefit when fathers talk about their wives. Your son is naturally curious about your relationship with your wife. He has an inherent need to understand where he came from and what series of events and combination of feelings caused you to marry and create him. This knowledge gives him a sense of security about his origins, and it also provides him with an understanding of men and women and how they fall in love. Therefore, don't be bashful about this topic. Although your wife also can talk to him about this, he will identify with the man's point of view. The following are some questions relating to your wife and the more general topics of love and women that can spark good conversations with your son.

- What are some of the things you have learned from loving and living with his mother?
- Why did you want to marry his mother? Explain how you proposed to her and where, the nature of the engagement, your wedding day, the honeymoon, and your first year of marriage. What was the wedding like?
- How important was your wife's love and acceptance of you as a father when your son was born?
- What attitudes have changed in your life toward women today?
- What initially attracted you to your wife?
- When you were a boy, how did you visualize marriage? Ask your son what he imagines his future wife will be like. What will she look like? What will she do for a living? How many kids will they have?
- How does your son see his relationships with girls/women as different from your own?

I realize that some of you may have a tense relationship with your son's mother. If you have gone through a bitter divorce or if you are in a troubled marriage, talking about some of the questions just listed may be off-putting. Nonetheless, I would advise you to have discussions with your son based on these questions and to be positive in your comments. If you have engaged in battles with your wife, your son has witnessed plenty of negative male-female interactions. It doesn't matter whether you feel you have acted appropriately or if your child's mother is the devil herself. You need to help him develop a balanced view of the opposite sex.

Perhaps the horse is already out of the barn, but if not, I would urge you to do everything possible to limit and manage the arguments you have with your wife. Constant bickering, verbal and physical battles, and hate-filled accusations and threats not only destroy marriages but also harm children. Kids are most affected by how parents fight rather than by what the fight was about. They concentrate on the displays of vitriol more than what is actually said. While every marriage has its arguments, they don't have to be lethal. If you agree in advance with your spouse that you will try to reach some sort of resolution at the end of every argument, you will have less of a negative impact on your child. Here is how a 14-year-old boy puts it: "I would be completely upset when I would hear my mom and dad screaming at each other. I didn't feel better until I would hear my parents make peace with each other. I never knew what they fought about, just how loud and mean they would get. Once they made up, I didn't worry any longer."

Parental arguing has emerged as a better forecaster of children's functioning than changes in the parent's marital status. Family systems researchers have found that high levels of marital conflict are more accurate predictors of children's behavior problems than is the family structure itself (e.g., marriage, divorce, blended family). I recognize that it is sometimes very difficult to manage the anger that emerges between a couple in a marriage because the friction that produces heated battles also creates romantic sparks. At the same time, you need to be conscious about this fighting. In other words, you should program an alarm to go off in your brain when you find yourself exchanging harsh words with your wife. To help you to set this alarm, let me tell you what this fighting does to boys.

Long-term exposure to a house full of tension undermines your son's sense of safety. It devalues his notion of self and reduces the chances for him to establish an emotionally balanced perspective. These ongoing battles form the relationship model that he will carry into all his future relationships and especially his romantic ones. Recognize, too, that when you bad-mouth your wife, you are bad-mouthing him. He is as much a part of her as he is of you, and your insults and invective wound him. In addition, your arguments require him to make an impossible choice: Who is right? He can't choose one side without rejecting the other. This is the type of reverse-Solomonesque decision that no child can make, especially a boy whose emotional intelligence is still forming.

Dealing with Divorce

This is an issue that seems to affect every couple, even though the current estimate is that one in two marriages ends in divorce. Couples may not divorce, but they may separate, have affairs, and otherwise damage the marriage, creating similar problems for children. It is also possible that you and your wife will not divorce but that you or she has come into the marriage after a divorce, bringing stepfathers and stepmothers into the parenting equation.

My concern is how men react to divorce, whether they are the ones involved in the divorce or if they are stepfathers. In either case, they can make mistakes that will cause their sons psychological harm. Girls, too, can be harmed by these actions, but in the majority of cases, mothers remain the primary caregivers after a divorce and maintain relationships with their daughters. The fathers are the ones who tend to leave, robbing boys of a male role model. Without a consistent male presence, boys experience a parenting vacuum and become vulnerable to acting out or repressing their emotions.

Divorce can't be prevented, but you can minimize its effect on your son. Before looking at the positive actions you can take, let's first examine the worst things dads do after a divorce:

- *See their children less frequently or not at all.* According to research conducted by Dr. John Gottman at the University of Washington (Seattle), dads actually increase their involvement with their sons in the first year after a divorce but steadily decrease their involvement in every subsequent year. In many cases fathers become discouraged after that first year, feeling that their ex-wives have become the dominant parent and that they have been shuffled aside. When ex-wives remarry, some dads feel as if they have been supplanted and voluntarily withdraw from the father-son relationship. Of course, some women deliberately encourage this withdrawal, attempting to use their children to punish their husbands for their misdeeds. Some women legitimately want to keep fathers away from their sons because of their physical and verbal abuse. Others, though, are furious with husbands who have had affairs and want to punish them by withholding or severely limiting visitation.

- *Fail to provide adequate financial support.* I am not going to go into a tirade about deadbeat dads; plenty has been written about this growing problem. Certainly there are instances when fathers can't afford to provide court-ordered support because they have lost their jobs and for other reasons. In some instances, though, men withhold support as their form of vengeance against ex-wives. Invariably, angry ex-wives tell their sons that they can't have a new bike or some other gift because "Your father didn't send the check this month." All this is terribly confusing to boys, especially younger ones. These acts communicate that "Your dad doesn't love you anymore."

- *Verbally abuse ex-wives.* You would think that men would know better than to tell their sons that their moms are harpies, whores, and other awful creatures. You would think that they would understand that as angry as they are at their ex-wives, they should not attack them in front of their sons, that by doing so their sons will feel confused by their fathers' attacks and feel as if they too are being attacked, and that their ex-wives will get wind of this verbal abuse and counterattack, calling dad all sorts of awful names. The verbal violence escalates, and sons are caught in the middle.

Stepfathers can also cause harm if they fail to step in when fathers step out. Biology does not make a father; empathy, involvement, and acceptance do. I am not suggesting that stepfathers usurp the role of biological fathers but rather that they take over some or all of the parenting responsibilities if the biological fathers aren't doing their jobs. Too often stepfathers feel that they don't have any authority—legal or emotional—with their wives' children. This is especially true when they become stepfathers of adolescents who often resent and disrespect them. They can still gain the respect and sometimes even the love of teenagers if they earn the authority. As difficult as teenaged boys can be, they often will warm up to stepfathers who listen without judging, offer advice without pontificating, and are fair without being pushovers. It takes time, but I have seen this transformation in attitude take place.

Certainly these are complex issues. Men sometimes flee from their children after a divorce because they are ashamed of failing as husbands. There are instances when fathers and stepfathers find themselves locked in a duel for a son's loyalty and affection, both of them sincerely believing that they will do a better job as a father and that the other person will do harm. I don't claim to have all the solutions to these complicated scenarios. I do know, however, that divorced fathers should do everything possible to maintain close, consistent relationships with their sons and that stepfathers should step into the breach if biological fathers give up on the relationship.

Raising Moral Boys in an Amoral World

As alluded to earlier, we live in a time when morality is no longer a big deal. The President of the United States commits an immoral act involving a White House intern, CEOs of companies are indicted left and right for insider trading and other irregularities, a famous professional baseball player is caught using an illegal corked bat, and a *New York Times* reporter is discovered to have invented parts of supposedly factual stories.

Helping your child to develop a strong sense of morals and solid values is challenging in this climate. It is very easy for boys to witness the hypocrisy that exists on the world stage and become cynical and amoral in their own lives. Many of their peers also may have adopted cynical attitudes, and this too influences their view of morality.

All you can do in response is to talk about and model moral behavior from the time your son is a little boy through young adulthood. Psychologist Lawrence Kohlberg has created a theory of moral development that suggests that this development is evolutionary—that boys act in "moral" ways to get rewards, to please dad, and to obey the rules. By the time boys reach adolescence, however, they begin to develop a deeper appreciation of morality and observe certain codes of conduct because they do not want to be seen as immoral people. The highest stage of morality is abstract moral understanding, and this occurs when boys learn to follow their principles not because of how society views their behaviors but to avoid self-condemnation; they don't want to commit an immoral act because they couldn't live with themselves if they did something like that.

You want to help your son reach this level of abstract moral understanding when he is an adolescent. Many boys don't reach these last two stages, getting stuck instead in earlier ones. There are adolescents and adults whose morality is limited to society's laws; they are moral only to avoid getting in trouble. If they feel they can commit an immoral act and not get caught, they will do so without a second thought.

To avoid having your son stuck in an early moral stage, you need to model moral behavior and talk with him about issues of morality, and you need to do so consistently and from the time he's a little boy. Too often dads commit small acts of immorality in their sons' presence that they view as insignificant. In fact, their sons—who watch everything their dads do with eagle eyes—will attach great significance to small lies and deceptions they observe. For instance, here are some examples of morally questionable actions dads commit while their sons watch:

- Promise someone on the phone that they will have something ready by Friday and then tell their wife, "There's no way it will be ready, but I've bought some time."
- Tell their sons that they will play catch with them when they get home from work but then decide to do something else, pretending they didn't agree to play catch.
- Brag about a clever scheme they have concocted that will save them money but that requires them to lie or deceive another person.
- Have an affair that their son hears about when the wife levels the accusation in his presence.
- Tell their wives that they will do the task they have asked them to do but then wink at their sons and whisper that they have no intention of doing it, making a joke out of it.

No one is Simon pure. Everyone tells a lie at one time or another. As a conscientious father, however, you need to be aware of the image you are presenting to your son and try to limit the number of instances when you say or do something that is morally questionable. Here are some basic ground rules to observe:

- When you make a promise to your son—no matter how small it seems—keep it. If you can't keep it, explain to him why you can't, and try to make it up to him at a later date.
- Don't brag about schemes and scams you have pulled off in your son's presence. This may be a necessary part of your job, but don't hold it up to your son as a positive aspect of it.
- Try to live by a consistent code of right and wrong. If you believe

that it is wrong to cheat, then don't do so when you are playing cards with your wife or a board game with your son. Let him see you living your moral beliefs, and don't confuse him with contradictory behaviors.

At a certain point, your son will be willing and able to engage you in discussions related to morality, and you should take full advantage of his interest. Although you can't talk him into being a moral human being, you can prompt him to think about issues of right and wrong, and this thinking process will help him to form his principles. Here are some easy ways to engage him in these discussions:

- When he is a preadolescent, use events that take place in school as catalysts. For instance, your son might come and tell you that another child tried to cheat off his test paper or that another boy was suspended from school for stealing someone's lunch money. Talk to him about how he felt about these situations. Why did he feel another boy did something wrong? What would have been the right thing to do and why?
- When he is a bit older—perhaps early adolescence—you can focus your discussion on something that happens in the news that involves morality. President Clinton's affair and Sammy Sosa's corked bat are two excellent examples. Ask him thought-provoking questions. Does he feel that President Clinton should have been impeached? Should Sammy Sosa be denied admission to the Hall of Fame after he retires?
- Watch for opportunities to talk about moral issues that involve shades of gray. Your son might tell you that one of his teachers who is gay devoted a class to a discussion of how and when people know they are gay and read excerpts from biographies of gay men that were mildly explicit. Shortly thereafter, the principal suspended this teacher. Talk with your son about whether he believes this was the right thing to do. This type of discussion can easily turn into a debate, which is fine. The goal is to encourage your son to explore his ideas about morality, and morally ambiguous subjects provide motivation for this exploration.

Transcending Fatherly Imperfection

As overwhelming as the challenges may seem at times, recognize that you are perfectly capable of meeting them. This is so because you don't have to be a perfect father to be a good one. In fact, expect to make mistakes in raising your son, just as your father made mistakes in raising you. These mistakes result in emotional wounds—ranging from small ones such as an unfeeling rebuke to big ones such as abuse. As painful as these wounds are, they can be overcome if you are conscious of how you were wounded and what you need to do to be a good father. In fact, these wounds can help you to become a better father, and they will help your son to be a better father, too.

At the time it is inflicted, of course, the wound hurts. Whether it's neglect or abuse or rejection or absence, it cuts to the quick of a boy. Over time, the wounds heal, and as boys grow into men, they learn to ignore the old hurts and even forget about them. This is when these wounds do the most damage. As we have seen, fathers who pretend that these wounds do not exist are the most vulnerable to their negative influence.

Addressing these emotional traumas from our boyhood, though, gives us a way to become more conscious as fathers and more compassionate toward our sons. When we think, talk about, and feel the wounds, we humanize our fathering. We become more patient and forgiving when we are emotionally in touch with ourselves, and the process of confronting and coming to terms with the hurt our fathers inflicted gives us the opportunity to get in touch.

Just as there is a physical benefit to feeling pain, there is an advantage to feeling the hurt of these emotional wounds. Just as touching a hot burner on a stove transmits a message of pain and triggers a reflex away from the burn to avoid more serious injury, the wounds from our childhood cause us to pull away from the more dangerous things we might do as fathers. To this end, I would like to share with you what I refer to as the *seven sins of fathering.* We all commit these sins. The goal, though, is to be sensitive enough to them because of the wounds we suffered as boys to avoid committing them too often. Here, then, are the seven sins:

1. *Act as though fathers don't matter.* If your father was absent or neglectful, you know how painful this sin can be for sons.

Don't convince yourself that mothers matter more than fathers. Don't demonize yourself as a bad father and tell yourself that your son would be better off without you. Fathers matter to sons, and the more you act like it, the more you'll matter to your son.

2. *Resent, hate, and be angry at your father.* If this is the glue that binds you to your father, it may very well be the glue that will connect you to your son. The other option is love. Getting stuck in hating your father hurts both relationships. You need to acknowledge the hurt he inflicted and move on. If your son sees you modeling a father–son relationship in which you are perpetually furious at your father, this is going to alter how he relates to you.

3. *Live in the past without being consciously aware of it.* As I emphasized in the first half of this book, the real sin of fatherhood is allowing the wounds of your boyhood to exert a negative influence on your parenting. Conscious fathering is the best type of fathering, and this means that you must examine whatever happened between you and your father when you were younger and come to terms with it.

4. *Blame your father for who you are today.* This is just fatalism in disguise. When you blame your father for your own flaws, you are essentially saying, "I'm not responsible for how I parent; it's my father's fault." Typically, the father who says this is suffering from shame and guilt from incidents that occurred between him and his father. You need to express your feelings about these incidents but stop holding your father responsible for how they shaped who you are. You are an adult who is now capable of taking responsibility for your own actions, especially as the father of a son.

5. *Uphold the male code of silence.* You don't communicate with your son, especially on an emotional level. You can rationalize your coldness a million ways to Sunday, but in the end, it is all about a myth your father and perhaps even his father subscribed to. This is a terrible legacy to pass on to a son, and you need to work on preventing your own son from inheriting it.

6. *Believe nothing will ever change between you and your father.* This belief represents depressed, hopeless thinking. Typically, dads

who commit this sin are overwhelmed by an emotionally or physically abusive childhood. This belief becomes a self-fulfilling prophecy, and it prevents you from creating an adaptable relationship with your own son. Father-son relationships can become tense, and resilient relationships accommodate this tension and allow both parties to move past it. Even if your father has passed away, you can still deal with the issues that separated you through increased awareness of the problems and how they have affected you. Just as importantly, most men are able to forgive their fathers' sins, freeing themselves from the hate they've harbored for years. Forgiveness must be part of every father-son relationship.

7. *Neglect your son.* This one sin encompasses a multitude of sins. Neglect can mean everything from failing to attend an event important to your son to not acknowledging his emotional needs. Fathers neglect their sons for all sorts of reasons, many of them rooted in the past. At some point in the future, they always regret their neglect.

Leave Your Son a Valuable Legacy

In the book's first chapter I asked you to imagine or remember your father's death. Now I would like you to do a similar exercise, only this time it involves imagining your own death and its impact on your son.

Visualize your son at your funeral. Picture the mourners circulating, the flowers, and the sadness. In the middle of this, focus on your son. Perhaps he is looking at your casket or your grave, and his thoughts are centered on you. With this image in mind, answer the following questions about your son:

- What is going through his mind at this minute?
- What would you like him to be thinking? Is there an experience you had together that you hope he is recalling?
- Is there an experience from your past that you wish had not happened and hope he doesn't dwell on?
- Is there something your son wishes had been part of the relationship between the two of you that never took place?

- As you are listening to his thoughts, is there one part of the script of your life together that you wish you could rewrite—a particular day, week, month, or year that you would change?

This exercise is designed to help you to change now what you won't be able to change in the future. The image of your own death should give you a clear picture of how you want your son to remember the relationship, and it should motivate you to adapt your parenting behaviors now so that this is how he will remember you.

All of you are at different stages as fathers and have different types of relationships with your sons. While I hope that they are generally good relationships, I also know that they can become bad. I realize that even if they are good now, there may be a crisis in the relationship at some point in the future. If things do become bad, I trust that what you have learned from this book will convince you that you should never give up on your son. He will always long for you as long as he lives. Even if you and your son haven't spoken in years or the relationship is strained, don't give up.

Instead, find your son and look at him as you did when you first fell in love with him when he was born. Or remember some incident from your shared past when an interaction between the two of you touched your heart. Or force yourself to swallow your pride and apologize. Whatever you do, make an effort to repair and rebuild a relationship that is tremendously valuable to both of you. Don't leave your son crying on your grave and asking why you never loved him.

You have the power to create a positive father-son relationship. You have the power to help your son grow into a successful, emotionally healthy young man and a caring, responsible father. To use this power effectively, communicate with your wife and rely on her for support and coparenting. Don't believe for a second that this power is diminished because you go through a divorce or because your son falls under the influence of a bad group of kids or drugs or because he does something immoral. You can help him through the worst adolescent crisis. As long as you resolve to be a conscious, involved father, he will become the son you always hoped he would be, and you will become the father he always knew you were.

Appendix 1

—◆◆ ◆◆—

Male Mythology Resources

M ANY OF MY PATIENTS find that it helps to view the father-son issue within a larger context. Fathers and sons often experience great emotional pain when dealing with the issues that lie between them, and more than one of my patients has remarked, "What's wrong with me?" Understandably, they feel as if they've made terrible mistakes or that the relationship they have with their own father or son is abnormal.

In most instances, the situations that arise are perfectly normal and even predictable. If you're going through these situations yourself, however, they seem anything but normal. When you find that you don't spend much time with your young son, or when you're engaged in battles with your teenager, it makes you feel as if you're the only one who is experiencing these feelings. You also may ask yourself, "Why does it have to be this way?"

The Bible certainly gives us evidence that father-son relationship problems go back thousands of years, but I prefer putting this relationship in a nonreligious, mythological context. Men who read books such as *Iron John* by Robert Bly or participate in men's groups often learn a lot about why they are the way they are from mythology. For this reason, I want to share with you how the father-son relationship and all the attendant problems are an integral and often necessary part of being male. I was tempted to include this material within the body of the book, but I decided to ground the book in prescriptive advice and psychological insight. Most men want to know what to do and why, and these were the book's focus. At the same time, I think that the following material will reassure you that you're not alone in your struggles as a father and as a son and that these struggles have a larger purpose in a boy's metamorphosis into a man.

The Three Horses

In mythology, different colored horses represent different stages in a man's life. Each color of the horse (red, white, and black) symbolizes a particular stage of growth and development from boy to man. Each stage is vitally important to a boy's ongoing development and long-term survival as a man. No stage can be skipped or overlooked. If a stage is missed, a boy suffers in some way.

In the following sections I'm going to relate the mythology of these three horses to the real issues that fathers and sons face. For those of you who aren't familiar with male mythology, be aware that it has its roots in an ancient, uncivilized world in which men were hunters and warriors. While our world has changed, the underlying impulses remain. Therefore, I'm asking you to "suspend your disbelief" much as you might do while watching a movie or reading a novel. In other words, don't take the mythology literally. Instead, accept it on its own terms, as a way of looking at familiar issues from an unfamiliar perspective. As I think you'll discover, it will open your eyes to what's taking place beneath the surface in both your life and that of your son.

What Is the Red Horse? Necessary Wounds and Defeats

Some religious and cultural traditions believe that no man is an adult male until he has become opened to the soul and the spirit world. If he doesn't open himself up, he will remain in perpetual adolescence. According to these traditions, such an opening can occur only through a wound in the right place, at the right time, and in the right company. *A wound allows the spirit or the soul to enter a boy's life.*

This is the red horse stage, a time of turbulence, aggressiveness, and troublemaking. Mothers, and other family members, as well as teachers, warn the boy to skip the red horse and go straight to the white horse, or civilized, stage. If a boy heeds this advice, he will return reflexively to the red horse later in life, becoming an obnoxious, "adolescent" 40-year-old. According to poet Robert Bly, "we [men] try these days to move young men by compulsory education directly from childhood into the White Knight" (*Iron John,* p. 206).

A boy enters the red horse stage at around age 15. Riding the red horse will continue until he is 30 to 35 years old. When a boy is in this stage, he will start showing his anger, fighting, and getting into trouble with male authority. The boy/young man will become arrogant, unreasonable, and hotheaded and will fight for what he believes in. Being passive isn't an option. The problem with the red horse stage is that boys need an older male—ideally a father—to guide them through the rage and pitfalls that arise from youthful mistakes. Many young boys become so consumed by rage, anger, and hostility that they lose sight of their life in the process. If their actions aren't monitored, directed, or discussed, they can turn fatal. It is the lack of involvement by fathers with their sons that makes this stage so dangerous and deadly.

We can see the most extreme examples of the red horse stage in street gangs. Many gang members don't have an involved father—they may not even know who their father is—and they manifest their red horse impulses with little or no restraint. At their root, however, even the gang shootings and other despicable acts have mythic justification. Gang members desire to act on perceived wrongs and protect what is rightfully theirs, similar to a knight in the Middle Ages or a Greek mythological hero. Gang bangers are men of action, and they harbor a sense of invincibility, recklessness, and fearlessness that would be char-acteristic of most mythic heroes. At the same time, these traits lead them to drugs, drinking, driving fast cars, and engaging in random sexual encounters. Boys have to feel their "blood boil," hunt down the enemy, and taste the power of victory and the deafening sound of defeat. All boys will have some degree of this "fire" in them. How they manage it depends on their father-son relationship.

I don't want to oversimplify this process. Getting on the red horse and entering into the black forest (the male adult world) involve a boy's relationship with his father, the unspoken permission from his father to leave home, and his level of pain and woundedness. Your son's journey on the red horse and into the forest reflects your own. If you haven't completed this journey properly, your son also will struggle with it. This is why many pages of this book have been devoted to helping you to deal with your own issues.

Even if you have dealt with these issues, though, you may still be shocked and dismayed by your son's behavior. When you put his behavior within the context of a warrior, though, what he's doing starts to make some sense and allows you to tolerate his wildness. In the red horse stage, many boys will move away from home, stop shaving, dress and look like another person, become disrespectful of their parents, drop out of school, lose their job, and date the "wrong" girl. Boys in this stage also will stop talking to their father and start smoking cigarettes, developing habits that are contradictory to their upbringing. These perceived acts of rebellion represent thousands of years of stored DNA pushing him to become a warrior. A warrior doesn't have to be violent, abusive of women, or an unlawful thug, but he may exhibit some noxious behaviors before he realizes this to be the case. Your son must establish that he is capable of taking care of himself in the forest (his world). Riding the red horse creates the warrior-type strength and mentality, providing him with an inner sense of competence, of being able to survive in his world, not yours.

The ends may not justify the means, but your son has a noble goal—becoming self-sufficient. Inner strength, courage, and confidence allow your son to move out of your house metaphorically. Your son will stay in the red horse stage until he develops the inner character qualities of mastery, direction (life purpose), and safety (can survive in the world). Sons who avoid the red horse process become young adults who still live at home and fear entering their black forest. They are afraid of growing up.

I realize that it's tough to view your son's obnoxious adolescent behavior as anything but pure selfishness and stupidity, but if you don't see the larger context for this behavior, you're likely to overreact and prolong the red horse stage. Consider, therefore, that the black forest in mythology has always meant facing the enemy, the giant, and the scary unknown. Only a brave warrior survived this trip into the forbidden area of his life and returned victorious. A true warrior or leader was chosen only after emerging from the forest, and there was always the possibility of being wounded or killed. The young warrior had to stay on his horse, get back on it after falling off, and return to the king's palace (the father's home). The return from the forest marked the maturing of the warrior who had survived his wounds from the battle. The warrior was on a mission to protect, preserve, and serve the king. Boys became men when they returned.

In more recent times, the military has served as a great vehicle for this rite of passage. Structured, male-dominated institutions have helped train boys into becoming warrior men, and sports has been a primary vehicle for achieving this goal. Football, especially, initiates boys into warrior rites of passage. A coach takes the role of the mentoring father, guiding, teaching, and allowing the young man to vent his inner fight.

The metaphor of home field is wonderfully illustrated in football. There is always a disadvantage to leaving your home field and going into the enemy's territory. Victory has to be achieved in the enemy's camp in order to have a successful team. The black forest is the enemy's field, and it has to be conquered. U.S. military history is filled with examples of successful campaigns in the enemy's homeland. Leaving your father's house and going into the black forest is considered entering enemy territory in mythology. Interestingly, most young warriors don't fight just physical battles but engage in emotional struggles with themselves. At some point on their journey they tackle whatever it is that is holding them back—fear, betrayal, guilt—and overcome it. It is only then that they can be truly triumphant. To protect his territory, the warrior must conquer the unknown territory at the edge of his country. Similarly, this young warrior learns not to allow anyone or anything to invade his mind, body, and psyche.

Now let's apply this myth to your present reality. Your son's internal emotional growth has to be fostered, and riding the red horse is the starting point of his process. If this horse/stage is skipped for any reason, he is unequipped for the natural separation from his father and mother. No boy can leave his father's home without the spiritual/emotional tools and the capacity to develop his soul. Leaving the father's house is a metaphor. Each boy needs the tools and support of his father to do it. For instance, moving away to college is a start. It is a step toward separation of a boy's heart and soul from his family. In the same way, this stage demonstrates why wise fathers advise their teenage sons not to marry. The emotional process to hunt and capture the prize cannot be cut short. Boys in this stage cannot be trusted because they are too angry and prone to fighting out their problems or disagreements.

The most relevant aspect of the mythology, however, involves a boy's wounds. These hurts can take many forms, from difficult family circumstances to fatherly negligence to all the pain involved in the normal process of growing up. Helping your son understand, endure, and eventually value the pain is how fathers can pave the way toward spiritual manhood and fatherhood. Your son will never grow up until he learns the hidden value of his emotional pain.

Chart Your Son's Battles, Wounds, and Monsters

One of the reasons I included this appendix was to give you a chance to apply male mythology to your son's life. On the surface, you may not view your son as anything resembling a warrior, especially if he's not involved in sports. It's difficult to imagine a quiet, book-reading science geek as a warrior. Nonetheless, this is exactly what he is, although he disguises it through his interests and personality. Underneath the surface, though, all boys are fighting battles, suffering wounds, and journeying through the forest.

Recognizing how this is so will help you to accept your son's journey and guide him through it. Try the following exercises in order to gain understanding of the mythological aspects of his journey:

Battle Exercise

1. List the "battles" your adolescent son has fought recently (or if he's older, recall ones that were memorable). Examples of battles might include
   - Fights with you or your wife over everything from money to the car
   - Disagreements with teachers over grades or other matters
   - Rivalries with friends in sports or over a girl
2. Describe the battle scene (either in writing or out loud to someone you trust) in terms of war; focus on how the battle started, the strengths and weaknesses of the combatants, and the outcome. For instance:

After school the other day, John (my son) searched for his algebra teacher until he found him in the teacher's lounge, surrounded by his supporters. John was furious that his teacher, Mr. Smith, had given him a failing grade despite John maintaining a B average, but despite Mr. Smith being in his own territory, John attacked him. Mr. Smith,

---

a loud, sarcastic teacher, had a natural advantage over John, who is shy and reserved. This time, though, John caught him off guard and let him have it. He showed Mr. Smith the report card and insisted the grade was unfair. Mr. Smith fired back that he received an F because he didn't turn in two homework assignments, and the rule in his class was that if two or more assignments weren't turned in, the student would receive an F. John fired back that he only missed one assignment, but Mr. Smith told him he was wrong and the F stood.

Wound Examination

1. List the different ways your son has been hurt recently. For instance:
   - Rejected by a girl when he asked her to the homecoming dance
   - Received a poor grade in a subject at which he tries very hard
   - Wasn't accepted into a summer program he applied for
2. Describe how your son expressed the pain of the wound (or if he seemed stoic on the outside).
3. How did the wound affect your son when he was faced with similar situations?

Monster Profile

1. Who is the main monster in your son's life? Is it you, your wife, a teacher, a bully at school, a coach, or a rival for a girl?
2. Describe this monster's strength and why he or she is a formidable opponent for your son. For instance:

Coach Dawson is an intimidator. He is a screamer, and he also is skilled at picking at a kid's weakness. He always accuses my son of being too nice to be a great football player, and my son is a nice kid. But my son feels that Coach Dawson goes too far and is unnecessarily cruel. He wants to stick it out with the team—he loves playing football—but he doesn't know if he can take Coach Dawson for much longer.

The White Horse—Civilized Men (Active Fathering)

The warrior enters the white horse stage when he returns from the black forest. He has fought and been wounded there, but he also has gone deep within himself and learned valuable lessons. In the mythology, a wise old man—in some cases, it's a wizard or other supernaturally wise being—often assists him on his journey through the black forest. Having survived his enemies and emerged from the forest, the boy is presented with a white horse.

This horse represents the "white knight," who is civilized and shining and gleaming with hope. He now fights for the good of humanity. He no longer fights impulsively or brims with aggression. He is concerned about the well-being of others and believes in the value of reconciling with others and forgiveness.

Communication, truth, relationships, and the Golden Rule now make sense in this white horse stage. No longer antisocial, rebellious, oppositional, or rude, the white knight represents his country, family, and son with the utmost of pride and confidence. There is a sense of protection and maturity in his approach to the people he loves and values. Integrity and the desire to solve any and all problems are some of his roles. This is a strong, compassionate, civilized son/man, not a wounded, bitter individual. He is at peace with the black forest.

As you might expect, the white knight is a highly desirable figure. Every mother wants her daughter to marry a white knight. He is liked by everyone and is the ultimate gentleman. The danger, of course, is that sons will hop on this white horse before they've completed the red horse stage. As a result, many phony white knights exist, pretending to be a white knight but not possessing the maturity to be this type of man. Many false white knights skip the red horse stage because they didn't have fathers to support them as they went through it. False white knights are insufferable, arrogant, and self-centered, and they use people and the world at large for their own personal gain. They lack compassion and understanding because they haven't gone through the red horse stage. The lack of battle experience has this son still looking for the enemy and always creating one. The phony white knight hasn't conquered his enemy and will create enemies in the workplace, at home, with his son, and with less fortunate people than himself. He is insincere and untrustworthy.

The genuine white knight is gracious to all the people he deals with. He understands the function and value of human interactions. He is able to mediate the issues that cause the red horse boys to fight each other. The treacherous white knight, on the other hand, exploits others and is considered more dangerous in mythology than the uncivilized warrior. The false appearance of being a civil and decent man is a disguise for the immature, scared, and preadolescent man.

The False White Knight Test

This mythology will help you to assess whether your son is in danger of becoming a false white knight. Answer the following questions to determine the degree of danger:

1. Were you and your spouse overly protective of your son, shielding him from anything that could hurt him?
2. Have you provided your son with relatively little advice and support—have you failed to be "the wise old man in the forest"?
3. Has your son steadfastly avoided any conflict with friends, teachers, and you?
4. Is he the type of kid who has always put on a show of being charming and courteous, almost as if he is acting a part rather than being himself?
5. Has he never participated in any sports?
6. Is your son extroverted but rarely introspective?
7. Are you a physically absent father?
8. Does your wife treat your son like the "perfect little boy" and encourage him to be different from all the other loud and unruly boys?
9. Does your son not have an enemy in the world?
10. Does it appear as if your son lacks emotional intelligence, that he finds it difficult to empathize with others and can only see things from his own perspective?

The odds are that you'll answer yes to at least one of these questions. Your son's vulnerability to false white knight status, however, increases if you answer yes to a majority of them. Remember that you can't protect your son from the wounds all boys suffer. What you can do, however, is be there for him when he needs your advice and emotional support. This will help him to move through the red horse stage and become a genuine white knight.

The Final Horse—Black Knight

Ideally, boys ride the red horse from adolescence until their mid-thirties. With maturity, they then ride the white horse until late middle age. The black horse is for the man over age 55 and for the rest of his journey in this life. I want to share information about this third horse with you because it provides a noble goal for all men. If we aspire to ride the black horse, we want to become true wise men. Let me describe what the black horse stage involves. The better you understand it, the easier it will be to focus on achieving this stage and helping move your son in this direction.

The black horse is the most powerful horse in mythology. Men riding on the black horse have given up blame and finger pointing. They have retrieved all the lost parts of their personality that they have thrown away at different stages of their life. This is a man who isn't given to naïveté, passivity, or numbness any longer. He is a man whom women of all ages want in their lives because he will answer their questions and address their concerns directly. There is no pretense or false bravado at this stage. The black knight isn't caught in the Peter Pan syndrome of never growing up and always fighting with his enemies. This is a man who has a sense of humor and the perspective on how to use it.

This is a man who avoids nothing, including the dark valleys of life. He isn't vain. Instead, he knows what is important in life. He is interested in understanding life's mysteries, the bigger picture, and helping his son and grandson along the path of fatherhood. This isn't the type of man who refuses to acknowledge his age or maturity. He has outlived fear and is now a mentor to younger sons looking to him for leadership, guidance, and support. The black knight is trustworthy because he embraces all the parts, pieces, and aspects of his life and is considered an evolved man by his peers.

In the terms of Jungian psychology, the black knight has eaten his shadow self and incorporated it back into his life. The shadow side that scares all men is accepted at this stage. You cannot ride this horse unless you come to terms with who you are; you must accept and embrace your previously perceived negative character traits. From a psychological perspective, this is the first stage of wisdom, which is considered the basic strength of senior adults.

The wise man, the old gray-haired man, is the black knight on the black horse. He teaches his son and the men around him how to give weight to their wounds consciously so that they will not lead an unconscious life. There is no sulking, pouting, or blaming his father for how things didn't turn out. He is accepting of the value of the painful, depressing experiences of his life. The black knight knows that without these growing experiences, he wouldn't be the man he is today. He has a sense of gratitude for how his life has evolved. The black knight understands the workings of the world and is very comfortable with the process of life.

In this stage, a man helps younger men grow and mature. He is a mentor who helps wounded, lost boys look inward and deal with the issues that have sidetracked them. This is a man who can talk to another man who is in a terrible state of grief and help relieve his pain and confusion. Dangerous, uncivilized sons and men fear the black knight because he is the only man who can expose their denial and defeat their terrorist approach to others.

Black Knight in Action—Conscious Fathering

My first encounter with a black knight was at the funeral for our Boy Scout leader's son, Jeff. Jeff was 3 weeks away from graduating high school. He was an Eagle Scout (the highest honor in scouting) and was driving home late on a Saturday night. His custom 1957 Chevy was hit head-on by another male driver, who was 16 years old and drunk. Jeff died immediately, and the drunk young male driver wasn't injured. I was 12 years old, and I went to the funeral with my best friend and fellow

Boy Scout buddy, Gregg. We didn't really know what was coming and how it would change both our lives.

When we entered the funeral chapel, all the other guys from our Boy Scout troop were walking up front to the open casket. I didn't realize that we were going to look at Jeff. The memory of seeing his face is as clear to me today as it was that day over 30 years ago. I saw for the first time the very thin line between death and life. All I remember after that was going to the burial site and watching Jeff's father throwing the first shovel of dirt on his casket. I couldn't stop crying. I remember thinking, "How do you bury your son?" while walking past his father, Mr. Barnes. Mr. Barnes stood there looking at us with the expression of a man who had seen this type of tragedy before. He was very present. I remember watching him nod and acknowledge the different people in the crowd, and he didn't even blink. I stared into his eyes as I walked by him on the grass at Forest Lawn Mortuaries; he had the look of a very wise man.

About 2 years later on a camping trip I asked Mr. Barnes how he was doing. I was trying to be a mature young man and never stopped wondering how he survived the death of his son. He replied, "I am fine, but are you okay now?" I don't remember what I said, but this was my first exposure to a black knight. Somehow he knew how scared I was of ever witnessing another father bury his son. I haven't seen Mr. Barnes in years, but he remains a true mentor and man in my mind.

Measuring Your Readiness to Ride the Black Horse

Most of you probably aren't old enough to ride the black horse. Nonetheless, it's never too early for white knights to start preparing themselves to become black knights. By focusing on the traits you need to acquire to change horses later in your life, you're starting to acquire wisdom that will help you be a better father to your son. While it's unrealistic to expect that you'll acquire all the wisdom necessary to be a black knight at this point in your life, you can work at being a wise white knight. To that end, I've created the following black knight wisdom measurement.

Black Knight Wisdom Measurement

Answer the following questions, recognizing that most of you won't be able to answer the majority of questions affirmatively.

1. When something goes wrong at work or at home, do you usually take responsibility for what went wrong rather than blaming others?
2. Do you find that you don't need to boast or play a role in order to impress others?
3. Do you rarely act childishly—having temper tantrums, getting in fights with siblings, being greedy?
4. Are you able to put problems and obstacles in perspective rather than becoming terribly upset when things don't go smoothly?
5. Are you aware of your Achilles heel? Do you accept and acknowledge your flaws and weaknesses?
6. Do people routinely turn to you for advice and support? Does your son?
7. Do you accept the disappointments of your life and move on (or are you constantly hung up on what went wrong and maintain that life is unfair)?
8. Do you feel grateful for your lot in life? Are you thankful for what you have? Do you feel blessed?
9. Are you willing to expose people whom you consider frauds? Do you sense that the phonies of the world shy away from you?
10. Are you a mentor to other men (including your son)? Do they turn to you in times of trouble and when they're grieving and need support?

Even if you can't answer a heartfelt yes to any of these questions, the desired, affirmative answers provide you with a barometer to gauge your wisdom. Just being aware of these questions will make you a more conscious man and ultimately a more conscious father. By trying to be the type of person who can answer these questions affirmatively— a man who feels grateful, who doesn't blame, who is emotionally supportive of others—you're naturally going to be a better father to your son.

Why Mythology Matters

The purpose of these mythological horses and knights is to illustrate the metaphorical process of becoming a father to yourself, to your son, and to the men in your life. We need these metaphors to help explain the yearnings in our heart to conquer the world, be a statesman, and be the wise, sought-after gray-haired man. There's a reason that just about every culture has created mythologies and passed them on from one generation to the next. Myths help people make sense of events that seem inexplicable. They provide a larger perspective from which to view problems and crises that befuddle us when we're enmeshed in them.

In mythology, there are larger purposes and more meaningful conflicts. Warriors battle monsters and face life-or-death struggles; there is nothing petty or insignificant in mythology. The mythological world isn't weighed down by the complexity and ambiguity of the real one. As a result, myths help us see the big issues played out on a grand stage. The three horses provide men with a sense of why we are the way we are in certain stages of our lives. We can see the logical evolution from red to white to black. In this context, the off-putting behaviors of our son make some sense, and our own journey as mentor and role model also provides coherence to events.

To grasp the value of mythology from a father's perspective, look at the following list of behaviors or attitudes that may be familiar:

- Son gets in fights
- Son is moody and uncommunicative
- Son argues about everything
- Son seems unfocused and unavailable to concentrate on anything.
- Son flits from one interest to the next but is unable to stick with one thing for any period of time
- Son spends a lot of time in his room listening to loud, irritating music
- Son challenges your ideas and values

Now translate your son's behaviors and attitudes into those of a young warrior in the red horse stage. Imagine if he

- Gets in fights with dragons and demons.
- Spends time meditating about his purpose and place in the world as he wanders through the forest.
- Stands up for himself when challenged by those who would thwart his journey through the forest.
- Focuses only on his survival and on outthinking or outfighting a given opponent.
- Moves from one place to the other in the unfamiliar forest, searching for his true home.
- Escapes from the stress of fighting and wandering by listening to the music of nature—the wind in the trees, the babbling of brooks, the songs of birds.
- Engages in debates with those he encounters about the best way to journey through the forest and reach safety.

The difference is that the latter scenarios are perfectly understandable within a mythic context. When you're a young warrior-hero on an epic journey, you're expected to get in fights and do other things that might not be normal in other circumstances.

Obviously, I'm not using this mythological example to suggest that you excuse or ignore your son's bad behaviors. I am simply asking that you view these behaviors within a context and learn to increase your tolerance of those which aren't dangerous to your son or others. By recognizing that your son's actions are part of a predictable process rather than anomalies, you'll gain a degree of patience and understanding.

The Double-Hearted Son

This process is also the pathway to creating a double-hearted son. This may sound like a mythological creature, but if you take the concept figuratively, you'll understand its application in your own life. The first heart is the natural, physical heart, and the second is the compassionate, soulful heart. Your son has to have a soul in order to develop and grow into the type of man, father, and partner who is a benefit to his own son.

From a mythological standpoint, sons develop a soulful heart through their own wounds. After being attacked by a wild beast, a dragon, or an enemy, the son experiences both pain and healing. He learns that he's not invulnerable, that despite his skills, knowledge, and bravery, he has weaknesses. From this point on, he knows what it's like to be hurt and can empathize with others who are wounded. The healing process provides him with the time and impetus to reflect and look inward. This wounding process is a painful but effective maturity catalyst. After being wounded, the warrior becomes more thoughtful and less action-oriented.

All this makes the young warrior—and you—a better father. Even if your wound was terrible—the result of physical abuse as a child, for instance—it can make you a stronger person and a more involved, supportive father. The key is looking inward, reflecting, and talking to your own father (or father figure) about it. Over time, you can use this wound to grow and develop the wisdom and compassion to help your son become double-hearted.

Appendix 2

—❯• ❮—

A Guide for Stepfathers
and Divorced Fathers

IF YOU'RE A STEPFATHER or a divorced dad not living with his son, you may have wanted more information than I was able to provide in the preceding pages. Although I tried to address the topic of blended families and the issues stepfathers and divorced dads face, I had to limit the discussion of this specific topic given all the other general topics I needed to cover. At the same time, I know that many of you are struggling with these issues, so I think you'll find this appendix helpful.

Let's start out with some facts. First, if you are a stepfather, recognize that not only aren't you alone, but you're also in the majority. It was estimated in 1990 by the U.S. Census Bureau that by the year 2000, more Americans would be living in stepfamilies than in traditional nuclear families. The U.S. Census Bureau was correct in its prediction for 2000, 67 percent of all families are either stepfamilies or some form of nontraditional family. The Census Bureau also predicts from its 2000 findings that at least 50 percent of all marriages will end up in divorce. This information isn't particularly new, but the implications are especially powerful if you're a dad with kids. There is a high statistical probability that if you're a dad, you will either marry someone who was married before or you yourself will experience a divorce.

I mention all this to communicate that to a certain extent we're in uncharted territory. Until relatively recently, these sorts of blended families were the exception rather than the rule. Now they're becoming the norm. Fathering a son is challenging enough without having the additional challenge of not living with your son or trying to be a father to a boy who isn't your biological son. The good news, though, is that I've found that men can do a great job of being a father in these challenging circumstances, especially if they have the right attitude.

A Father Is a Father Is a Father

The advice of the preceding pages still holds, even if your son doesn't live with you or that the boy you're raising doesn't call you dad. If you're the primary adult male figure in his life, you need to understand your issues with your own dad and work hard at being an involved and emotionally supportive father.

It's also critical that you don't use your nontraditional family circumstances as a cop-out. Too many stepfathers or divorced fathers make excuses for themselves as dads, claiming that their ex-wives or their boys' relationship to biological dads makes their role meaningless. This becomes a self-fulfilling prophecy. If you convince yourself that you don't have the capacity to be a father to your son, you'll unfortunately be right.

Therefore, start out with a positive attitude. I've seen men in extremely difficult family circumstances who shine as dads. It may well be that your ex-wife bad-mouths you in front of your son or that your stepson is furious at both his mother and you for separating him from his "real" dad. If, however, you make a commitment to being a loving, present father to your son, you're likely to find that your efforts will pay off in a mutually rewarding relationship. Keep in mind that boys desperately need a father figure in their lives, and the instinctive desire of a boy for this father-son relationship usually overcomes whatever obstacles other people or circumstances throw in the way.

To keep the right attitude, take a look at the following excuses dads make about why they can't be the fathers they want to be:

- My ex-wife has poisoned my son's mind against me.
- Ever since the divorce, my son hasn't wanted anything to do with me; he blames me for breaking up the family.
- I don't get to see my son enough (because of the custody agreement) to form a real relationship with him.

- My son likes his stepfather more than he likes me.
- I'm just his stepfather, so I can't have a real father-son relationship with him, even though his father isn't around much.
- As a stepfather who has never had kids of his own, I don't really know how to be a father.
- I've got three other biological children to parent; I'll leave my stepson to his mother.
- This is my third marriage and my wife's second; I can't be a father to all the kids.

Don't give in to this excuse making. Whether you're a divorced father or a stepfather, you can have a profoundly positive influence on your son if you don't dwell on all the reasons why you can't have this influence. Yes, you may have to work harder at it, but you have many ways to make the relationship work, even when there has been a difficult divorce.

Divorce—Staying Involved

Divorce changes all family relationships, not just the one between husband and wife. Children are affected in many different ways, and the impact is especially pronounced regarding the noncustodial parent. When a parent who has been a constant in the child's life moves out, the child can feel angry, resentful, guilty, and jealous. The child's feelings are exacerbated when the tension between his parents escalates because of financial disagreements or other conflicts. In addition, children become angry or confused (depending on their age) when mom or dad starts dating. Because dads are usually the noncustodial parent, they're often the ones whose relationships with their kids deteriorate first and most significantly.

While you don't have control over some of these issues, you can be aware of how a given situation is affecting your son. Don't put on blinders and assume that he'll be fine just because he's a good kid with good values. You need to be extra sensitive to his feelings and do everything possible to avoid causing him unnecessary pain because of the divorce (remember, he's going to have plenty of wounds to deal with on his own). At the very least, you need to be attuned to how he's reacting to various postdivorce situations and make an effort to talk with your son and your ex-wife about them. While these conversations aren't always easy, they're easier than watching your son drift away from you.

Just as the quality of a marriage affects the father-son relationship, the quality of a divorce has a similar impact on the relationship. In a bad divorce—one that involves continuous verbal arguments between the divorced couple, ongoing legal fighting, or a parent (or parents) who talks about his or her spouse in negative terms—kids tend to draw away from one or both parents. In bad divorces, dads often are so distraught about what's going on that they withdraw from the relationship. They're torn between their legal and relational obligations and the desire to flee from the shame of a failed marriage. These bad divorces often create fatherless sons.

Frequently, even the most concerned, caring dads feel like giving up. This often happens when a man's ex-wife forms a new relationship. It may be that she remarries, has another child, and starts building a new family life. In this situation, dads often feel left out. They may believe that their sons love their "new" fathers better than them, that they don't have a chance of "competing" because they only see their sons on weekends and the stepfathers see them every day of the week, and that the new family seems genuinely happy—far happier than when they were living with their wives and sons. In these instances, dads often have an overwhelming desire to cut themselves off from the family, including their sons. It's not that they don't love their children. Instead, they often feel that their kids would be better off without them. Or they believe that the stepfathers can do a better job of being a father than they could.

As difficult as it may be, you need to resist the impulse to end relationships or even reduce your involvement. Although it may be painful to be a visitor in your own house or to believe (falsely) that your son loves his new father better than he loves you, hang in there. Sooner or later, things will get better. It may be that you remarry and start a new family and no longer feel like the odd man out. It's possible that over time your relationship with your ex-wife will improve—sometimes the bitterness that is so intense in the period right after the divorce diminishes with time. In some instances, financial situations improve, reducing the stress on everyone.

Remember, your relationship with your son depends on your involvement, even if that involvement initially is painful to both you and him.

It's Not What You Argue About, It's How You Argue About It

Family systems theory has proven that how you argue with your partner rather than the subject matter determines marital longevity. This theory also suggests that how adults fight matters more to children than what the fight is about—this is true whether a couple is married or divorced. Kids are more distressed by conflict that is angry, physical, and continually unresolved than by marital status. Even loud displays of anger can be less toxic and damaging if you and your partner end the conflict by communicating that you've reach a resolution. Although you may not feel like kissing and making up after an argument with your ex, attempting to end the argument on a note of resolution makes kids feel much less threatened by the hostility that flared during the argument.

The nature of arguments is a better forecaster of children's functioning than changes in the parent's marital status. In other words, family systems researchers have found *that high levels of marital conflict are more accurate predictors of children's behavior problems than is the family structure itself (marriage, divorce, or blended family).* This is very valuable to fathers in or out of a marriage; arguing and chronic tension with your partner are highly unproductive for your son. Long-term exposure to a house full of tension undermines your son's sense of safety, devaluing his sense of self and reducing the chances for an emotionally balanced perspective. The ongoing fighting with your son's mother becomes the relationship model that he will carry into all his future relationships and especially his romantic ones.

In the final chapter of this book I touched on this subject, but here I want to go into a bit more depth about why fighting has such a negative impact and recommend a number of specific tactics that will help fathers to avoid the worst types of arguments and reduce their number.

To help you to make a commitment to avoid vicious, unresolved arguing with your ex-wife, think about what is going on in your son's mind and heart when you argue. Ongoing nuclear encounters with your son's mother expose him to inner conflict, fear, and emotional instability. When a father bad-mouths his son's mother, he is bad-mouthing part of his own son. The shortsighted arguing and pattern of verbal abuse are the equivalent of exposing your son to nuclear radiation. In many cases boys (especially under the age of 10) personalize a divorce and blame themselves for the breakup. Boys are also more self-critical and self-loathing when their parents exhibit a high level of tension, anger, and conflict. The long-term effects of this fighting will be apparent in your son's life many years down the road. To the degree that you can contain and redirect your feelings of resentment, rage, and disappointment and sense of failure and keep it from open displays in front of your son, it will greatly benefit your father-son relationship. You can stop the cycle of arguing. There are many creative ways to communicate with your son's mother that aren't hostile or aggressive. Your ability to avoid argument in front of your son or in private will help him with the other challenges. Recognize that while your son may survive the divorce without any long-lasting psychological harm, he may not survive chronic arguing and rage without being adversely affected. Sons learn to imitate their father's behavior, and this isn't the behavioral model you want him to follow.

Tension-Diffusers and Peacemaking Tips

Learning how to argue fairly and cleanly is something that will benefit your relationship with both your son and your ex-wife. Even if you and your ex fought like caged animals during the divorce, you can learn to disagree civilly and constructively afterwards. Your primary job after a divorce is to devote your full attention to the business of fathering. This is difficult to do if you remain enmeshed in an endless argument syndrome. It takes energy to engage in battles with an ex, and these battles often will leave you drained and dispirited. It's difficult to be a good father to your son under these circumstances. Remember, you might be an ex-husband, but you are never going to be an ex-father. Therefore, prioritize establishing a civil relationship with your ex-wife or else you're going to start feeling like an ex-father.

The way you decide to divorce is strongly influenced by the quality (or lack thereof) of your marriage. A cynical truism: What makes a good divorce is a good marriage. The implication here is that if there was any degree of trust, respect, good will, and cooperation around raising your son prior to the divorce, there (eventually) will be later on as well. Obviously, if you had a lousy marriage from the start and you and your wife constantly argued about how to raise your son, then this will carry over into the postdivorce relationship. The odds are, though, that at one point you had a good marriage. Perhaps early on you shared a similar parenting philosophy with your wife and worked well together as parents. What you want to do is recapture the good will and shared parenting beliefs. Make an attempt to focus on your shared beliefs and values as parents, and use those to guide your discussions. If you both believe in the value of a private-school education, keep that value in mind as you discuss who will pay for this education rather than on making accusations about how "your decision to file for divorce makes a private school impossible." Your values and beliefs are powerful, and if you and your ex-wife share them, they can help you to make decisions and discuss problems without rage or recrimination.

The good news is that you can take proactive steps to decrease the odds of hostile encounters with your ex-wife. Here are some steps that my clients have found to be effective and that can be put into place the moment the relationship ends:

- *If you are leaving/moving out, tell your son that you're going to leave when your wife is present.* You two made this boy together, and he needs to know that you two aren't divorcing him. Hard as this may be for you, a joint effort will reassure your son that both of you want him to be an integral part of your lives. You don't need to go into great detail about the reasons you're leaving, but you do have to reassure him that you both will always love him and be there for him.

  Frequently, these leave-takings are acrimonious affairs, with husbands and wives screaming at and blaming each other. This sets the tone for postdivorce communication. For years afterwards, this leave-taking is held up by one or both people as an example of how the other person messed up. It also is a traumatizing event for a boy to witness.

Therefore, deal with this moment with compassion and consideration for your son rather than anger toward your wife. Make her part of the process of saying good-bye.

- *Don't talk about the financial conditions of the divorce with your son.* Many men are terribly resentful about the amount of support they have to pay their wives or how the property was divided. When they talk about these issues, they can't keep the anger and bitterness out of their voices. Even if you think you can control your words and tone of voice when discussing this subject with your son, the odds are that he'll quickly discern your resentment. If you talk about how much you're paying his mom, he's likely to tell her you told him, and this invariably will lead to a ferocious argument. She'll accuse you of making it seem like she's bleeding you dry, and you'll accuse her of not disclosing to your son that you haven't left him or her high and dry.

  It's fine to talk about nonfinancial custody issues, since your son will want to know when and how often you'll be seeing him. Just steer clear of the financial details. If you disclose them, they'll get back to your wife and trigger a nasty fight.

- *Set up a temporary/standard custody and regular visitation arrangement before you leave.* I realize that this may not be what your lawyer tells you to do and that you may be so consumed by anger as you're packing your things that you feel you can't even think rationally about custody and visitation. Nonetheless, this action is not only in the best interest of your son, but it's a good way to reduce a source of tension between you and your wife. From your son's standpoint, he is anxious about when he'll see you and how often, and if you can reduce his anxiety, it will help you both to get past the sadness and pain of the family breaking up and resume the relationship on solid ground. From a tension standpoint, be aware that arguments over these issues are common. Typically, your wife will complain that you don't seem to make time for your son. Or you'll complain that she doesn't allow you to see him enough. There will be miscommunication about who picks him up when, and there will be instances when you have your heart set on taking him to a particular event and she'll say no.

The more you establish mutually agreed-on guidelines from the start, the less likely that visitation and custody issues will be sources of bitter, divisive arguments. Certainly you'll disagree with your wife about these issues in the months and years to come, but establishing guidelines from the start diminishes the intensity of these arguments. If you can agree on the basic principles, then you'll just be disagreeing about the details, which tends to be a less explosive topic.

- *Make an effort to know as much as possible about your son.* Again, this is beneficial for you and your son and for the relationship with your ex-wife. If your son feels that you're aware of what's going on in his life, he'll be much more receptive to spending time with you. Some dads, though, lose touch with their kids after they move out. Obviously, if you're not in your son's presence on a daily basis, it's more difficult to keep up with the changes in his life. Therefore, you need to make an effort to find out what's going on with him at school, if he's started new hobbies or dropped old ones, if he's made a new group of friends, and so on. Many husband/ex-wife arguments start when the dad says something like, "Isn't Joey supposed to go to swimming lessons today," and the mom replies, "Joey stopped those lesson 8 months ago, which shows how much you care about him."

- *Treat your son as if he's family and lives with you all the time.* Really, this is all about your attitude. Your son can read you well, and if you start treating him more like a nephew you're fond of rather than the son you love, he'll notice the difference. He also may comment to his mother that you seem distant or different in some way, and you can be assured that his mom will bring this up to you. The odds are that you'll react defensively, and an intense argument will ensue.

- *Be civil and circumspect in your dealings with your son's mother.* I know that I've said this before, but it bears repeating because it's often a major challenge for fathers to be civil and circumspect. Even if you feel that your wife is manipulative, duplicitous, greedy, and all the other negative adjectives you can think of, make the effort to treat her with respect. Keep in mind that this is not about her or you but about your son, and if you attack her, she'll attack you, and your son will feel as if his presence has destroyed your relationship. He'll hear you arguing about him and feel that he's to blame for the animosity between you; and if you and your wife do a good job bad-mouthing each other, he eventually may believe that both of you are unworthy of his respect.

Try to help your ex-wife be the best mother she can be for your son. This means supporting her decisions whenever possible and reminding your son about her good qualities. It also means avoiding criticisms and complaints about her. Specifically, don't

- Use the time with your son to list all your grievances against his mother
- Accuse your wife of breaking up the family and claim that you wanted to stay married
- Tell your son how you knew from the start that it was a mistake to marry her
- Blame your wife for not being able to see your son as much as you would like
- Side with him when he tells you that his mother won't let him stay out late, get a toy, and so on
- Tell him that things would be different if he lived with you
- Share secrets about his mom that he can use as leverage to get what he wants
- Encourage him to disobey his mother
- Explain that you're paying enough in support that she can afford to get him whatever he wants
- Discuss in detail all the problems in the marriage to help him see why it was not going to work
- *Form a parental alliance with your ex-wife for your son's benefit.* The operative words in this alliance are *cooperation, support,* and *communication.* This process will take time, but it is worth the effort for your son's emotional, mental, and physical functioning. Fathers who are able to communicate with their sons' mothers report a much higher degree of satisfaction and emotional connection with their sons. Just as significantly, they're less likely to engage in the battles that alarm and alienate sons.
- *Show up.* Woody Allen once said that 80 percent of success was just showing up. The same holds true if you're a divorced dad.

You're allocated a certain amount of time with your son, and you should do everything possible not to miss a second of it. There are going to be times when you're down or you feel that you need to work or when someone invites you to do something fun, but your time with your son always should take priority. Men who don't show up earn the ire of their ex-wives, and for good reason. In the short run, this schedule may mean that you have to give up some things. In the long run, it means that you'll get tremendous satisfaction out of the relationship with your son.

- *Avoid the Disneyland father syndrome.* In other words, don't try to buy your son's love with trips, gifts, and tickets to rock concerts and sporting events. I've seen too many dads substitute things for expressions of love. If you're falling into this pattern, you're probably doing so to escape the sadness that both you and your son feel. It doesn't work. In addition, your former spouse is likely to resent this type of spending, especially if she's having financial problems. All you really need to do is *be* with your son. Talk to him, eat with him, play catch with him. This is more than enough activity to establish a meaningful connection.

- *Follow a routine.* Routines provide the stability your son craves, and they also allow you to avoid scenes with your ex-spouse when you show up at unexpected times or miss scheduled visits. Perhaps every weekend you might schedule a breakfast with your son at the same time and place. Or if you have a younger son, you might play a game every time you visit on a certain day. Perhaps you make a habit of doing certain chores together with your son. Whatever the routine is, adhere to it.

- *Be smart about and prepared to deal with the family law business.* This doesn't mean getting a great divorce lawyer and trying to figure out how you can punish your wife. It is about being reasonable and trying to resolve issues without lawyers or court appearances. There are instances when lawyers are necessary, but the less you use them, the less costly and adversarial the process is. The last thing you, your wife, or your son need at this point is huge legal expenses; they can add even more stress to an already stressful situation. A pitched legal battle over custody, visitation, or property can create animosity for years to come. Therefore, never, ever use the legal system for vengeance. Always try to work things out with your son's mother rather than your ex-wife; this perspective will make it easier to compromise and treat her with respect.

- *Learn to manage conflict with skill.* Over 50 percent of divorced mothers/wives admit to interfering with the father's custody and visitations (Father Source Network 2002) with their children. Therefore, expect your ex-wife to tinker with your visitation schedule, cut short some visits, and offer reasons why your son can't be with you on a given weekend. She may have legitimate reasons for interfering with your schedule, or she may be doing it for vindictive purposes. It really doesn't matter why she's doing it. What's important is how you handle it. Conflict-management skills revolve around the ability to reflect before reacting and compromise before condemning. Bend over backwards to consider her point of view. You may not agree with it, but you may appreciate it, and that will allow you to discuss an issue with her without vitriol. Try to find middle ground when you have disagreements rather than digging into your position. If she seems deliberately antagonistic, swallow your pride and try to defuse a tense situation. All this may not be particularly satisfying, but it generally is what's best for your son.

- *Create your own supportive network.* One good way to keep the peace with your son's mother is to establish a group of men and women who will provide you with emotional and informational support. There are times when you're going to need to vent, and this network can give you an outlet for all the anger that's boiling up inside you. It also can connect you with other men who are going through the same things you are, and their empathy will help you to get through the most difficult postdivorce periods without blowing a gasket. You may want to join a divorced men's support group or include a therapist in your network. The key is not to go it alone, for your sake and for that of your son.

I realize all these tips may not seem like much of a defense when your ex-wife wants to change the terms of the custody arrangement, demands more support, or reneges on an agreement that you could take your son on a weekend camping trip. No matter what you do, you still will become furious at times. If you can control that fury and limit your ex-wife's exposure to it, though, you'll find that your son and your relationship with him benefit. These tips are really survival skills for divorced dads. They may not eliminate some of the postdivorce problems you'll experience, but they'll allow you and your son to tolerate them with less destructive effects. This may not seem like a lot, but over the long haul it will facilitate better communication with your ex-wife and make it easier for both of you to make decisions that benefit your son.

Stepfathers Stepping In

If you're a stepfather as opposed to a divorced dad (of course, you also can be both), you need to deal with your own insecurities about becoming an "instant" father as well as your stepson's potential animosity toward you. Some stepfathers respond to their new role by being too fatherly, overwhelming boys who don't know how to deal with their intense attention. Other stepfathers retreat from the role of parent, fearing that they're not up to the job or avoiding their stepson's hostility.

To help you to become the stepfather your wife's son needs, let me share the story of how one man handled this new role.

Thomas is an 8-year-old boy who sees his father about once a month. His mother, Debbie, is the primary parent in his life since the divorce 5 years ago. Thomas misses his father, Charles, who has moved approximately 2 hours away. Debbie met a wonderful man, Tim, who lives 5 minutes away from her. Tim over the last 2 years has met Thomas and developed a very strong relationship with him. Tim and Debbie recently got married, and Thomas was in the wedding. Now, with all three people living together and creating a new family, there have been some adjustments to make.

Thomas is now 8 and doesn't remember ever living with his father. Debbie is 35 and would like to have another baby before her biological clock runs out. Tim and Thomas both think a baby would be great, but they also feel that they should get to know each other better before making matters even more complicated. Thomas loves Tim but has some difficultly sharing his mother all the time with her new husband. Thomas has always been the main man in his mother's house, and he doesn't like being displaced by another man. At the same time, Thomas also craves an involved father, and Debbie is eager to facilitate the relationship between Thomas and Tim.

Tim and Debbie have been very conscious about how they would establish their stepfamily and highly sensitive to Thomas's needs and concerns. For instance, the first meeting between Tim and Thomas was at a Dodger baseball game. Tim drove to Dodger Stadium himself and met Debbie and Thomas there. Tim only stayed for four innings. Since baseball is Thomas' favorite sport, Debbie thought it would be easy for him to meet Tim in this setting. Limiting the time together to four innings prevented the encounter from being too overwhelming for Thomas. After that initial meeting, they increased the time Tim and Thomas spent together in increments until they were comfortable together. Once that comfort level was reached, Tim and Thomas began doing some things together without Debbie.

This type of step-by-step acclimation is just one tactic that helps a stepfather take on his new role in a way that fosters a strong stepfather-son relationship. Let's look at some other tactics that should be helpful in this regard:

- *Reach agreement about the house rules.* In other words, don't create the impression that you're issuing orders and taking over. Your stepson needs to understand that you and his mother are acting in concert. When you must discipline him, he should recognize that you have the complete support of his mom. Work out this issue prior to marriage because it can be a deal breaker. How do you want your stepson raised? How does your new wife want her son raised? These two questions are the foundation for a solid family unit. While it's impossible to anticipate every problem or decision, you can set some basic ground rules that will cover the majority of issues that arise.
- *Don't allow your son to divide and conquer.* This is a corollary to the preceding tactic. Children are great at causing mom and dad to take opposing positions. This isn't allowable in a new family. The enduring strength of the couple is the ability to be unified as a team. The boy will accept you and his mom as a couple much

sooner when you present a united front than when you are at odds with each other.

- *Don't minimize your role as a stepfather.* From an emotional standpoint, boys don't discriminate between stepfather and father, which are artificial labels. Being a father is being a father. Your new son will bond with you based on the love, support, interest, and attention that you give his life. Therefore, be involved. Resist the impulse to fade into the shadows where your stepson is concerned, deferring to his "real" father, your wife, grandparents, and others. Recognize that your role is important and that you diminish that importance by separating yourself from your stepson.

- *Teach the five R's—respect, rules, roles, responsibilities, and realistic expectations.* Your new son may not like you at first, but he can learn to be respectful. With your wife, determine the house rules, your son's responsibilities, and you and your wife's responsibilities. In addition, specify your expectations. Do you expect him to clean his room each day? Does he expect you to attend his Little League games? This will reduce the disappointment when expectations aren't met, as well as cut down on the fights and other negative actions when rules are broken or responsibilities are shirked because they weren't clearly defined.

- *Never bad-mouth your stepson's birth father publicly.* It may be that this birth father is a physically abusive, drug-using jerk. Nevertheless, you should not refer to him as a jerk in front of your stepson. Sons are loyal to their fathers even when there's no rational reason why they should be. Respect your stepson's feelings. By being a good person and a good role model, you're essentially communicating the message that his biological father is not a good model, but you're doing it in a way that won't make him angry at you.

- *Adore and respect your new wife in front of her son.* It is a huge relief when a son sees his mother in a loving, nurturing, supportive relationship. Even though he may not seem relieved initially, he will be grateful for your loving, respectful attitude. This is especially true if your predecessor was abusive. By treating your wife with love and respect, you're also modeling for your stepson how women should be treated, a lesson he may not have learned from his biological father.

Bibliography

Allen, Patricia, and Harmon, Sandra. *Getting to I Do. The Secret to Doing Relationships Right*. New York: William Morrow, 1994.

Biddulph, Steve. *Raising Boys. Why Boys Are Different—and How to Help Them Become Happy and Well-Balanced Men*. Berkeley, CA: Celestial Arts, 1998.

Biller, Henry B., and Trotter, R. J. *The Father Factor. What You Need to Know to Make a Difference*. New York: Pocket Books, 1994.

Blankenhorn, David. *Fatherless America: Confronting Our Most Urgent Social Problem*. New York: HarperCollins, 1995.

Bly, Robert. *Iron John: A Book About Men*. Reading, MA: Addison-Wesley, 1990.

Bray, James H., and Kelly, John. *Stepfamilies: Love, Marriage, and Parenting in the First Decade*. New York: Random House, 1998.

Brazelton, T. Berry. *Working and Caring*. Reading, MA: Addison-Wesley, 1992.

Canada, Geoffrey. *Reaching Up for Manhood: Transforming the Lives of Boys in America*. Boston: Beacon Press, 1998.

Covey, Stephen R. *The Seven Habits of Highly Effective Families*. New York: St. Martin's Griffin, 1997.

Deida, David. *The Way of the Superior Man: A Spiritual Guide to Mastering the Challenge of Work, Women, and Sexual Desire*. Austin, TX: Plexus, 1997.

Dobson, James C. *The New Hide or Seek*. Grand Rapids, MI: Revell, 1999 (1974).

Estes, Clarissa P. *Women Who Run with the Wolves*. New York: Random House, 1992.

Gallo, E., Gallo, J., and Gallo. K. *Silver Spoon Kids: How Successful Parents Raise Responsible Children*. New York: McGraw-Hill, 2001.

Garbarino, James. *And Words Can Hurt Forever: How to Protect Adolescents from Bullying, Harassment, and Emotional Violence*. New York: Free Press, 2002.

Garbarino, James. *Lost Boys: Why Our Sons Turn Violent and How We Can Save Them*. New York: Simon & Schuster, 1999.

Garbarino, James. *Parents Under Siege: Why You Are the Solution, Not the Problem in Your Child's Life*. New York: Touchstone Books, 2002.

Garbarino, James. *Raising Children in a Socially Toxic Environment*. San Francisco: Jossey-Bass, 1995.

Gilligan, J. *Violence: Our Deadly Epidemic and Its Causes*. New York: Putnam, 1996.

Gottman, John. *Raising an Emotionally Intelligent Child*. New York: Simon & Schuster, 1997.

Gurian, Michael. *A Fine Young Man: What Parents, Mentors, and Educators Can Do to Shape Adolescent Boys into Exceptional Men*. New York: Tarcher, 1999.

Gurian, Michael. *Boys and Girls Learn Differently: A Guide for Teachers and Parents*. San Francisco: Jossey-Bass, 2001.

Gurian, Michael. *The Good Son: Shaping the Moral Development of Our Boys and Young Men*. New York: Tarcher, 1999.

Gurian, Michael. *The Soul of the Child: Nurturing the Divine Identity of Our Children*. New York: Atria Books, 2002.

Gurian, Michael. *The Wonder of Boys. What Parents, Mentors and Educators Can Do to Shape Young Boys into Exceptional Men*. New York: Putnam, 1996.

Harris, J. R. *The Nurture Assumption: Why Children Turn Out the Way They Do.* New York: Free Press, 1998.

Keen, Sam. *Fire in the Belly: On Being a Man.* New York: Bantam Books, 1991.

Kimmel, Michael. *Manhood in America: A Cultural History.* New York: Free Press, 1996.

Kindlon, Dan. *Too Much of a Good Thing: Raising Children of Character in an Indulgent Age.* New York: Hyperion, 2001.

La Rossa, Ralph. *The Modernization of Fatherhood: A Social and Political History.* Chicago: University of Chicago Press, 1997.

Leman, Kevin. *What a Difference a Daddy Makes.* Nashville: Thomas Nelson, 2000.

Levine, Suzanne B. *Father Courage: What Happens When Men Put Family First.* New York: Harcourt, 2000.

Loeber, R., and Farrington, D. P. *Serious and Violent Juvenile Offenders: Risk Factors and Successful Interventions.* Thousand Oaks, CA: Sage, 1998.

Lofas, Jeannette, CSW, and Sova, Dawn B. *Step Parenting: The Family Challenge of the Nineties.* New York: Kensington Books, 1985.

MacKenzie, Robert J. *Setting Limits: How to Raise Responsible, Independent Children by Providing Reasonable Boundaries.* Rocklin, CA: Prima Publishing, 1993.

Moore, Thomas. *Care of the Soul.* New York: HarperCollins, 1992.

Oh, Kara. *Men Made Easy: How to Get What You Want from Your Man.* Berkeley, CA: Avambre Press, 1999.

Osherson, Samuel. *Finding Our Fathers: How a Man's Life Is Shaped by His Relationship with His Father.* New York: McGraw-Hill, 1986.

Osherson, Samuel. *Wrestling with Love: How Men Struggle with Intimacy, with Women, Children, Parents, and Each Other.* New York: Random House, 1992.

Parke, Ross D., and Brott, Armin. *Throw-Away Dads: The Myths and Barriers That Keep Men from Being the Fathers They Want to Be.* Boston: Houghton Mifflin, 1999.

Pollack, William. *Real Boys.* New York: Henry Holt, 1995.

Pruett, K. D. *Fatherneed: Why Father Care Is as Essential as Mother Care for Your Child.* New York: Simon & Schuster, 2000.

Real, T. *I Don't Want to Talk About It: Overcoming the Secret Legacy of Male Depression.* New York: Scribners, 1997.

Rolfe, Randy. *The 7 Secrets of Successful Parents.* Chicago: Contemporary Books, 1997.

Shapiro, Jerold L. *The Measure of a Man: Becoming the Father You Wish Your Father Had Been.* New York: Berkley Publishing Group, 1995.

Zax, Barbara, and Poulter, Stephan. *Mending the Broken Bough: Restoring the Promise of the Mother and Daughter Relationship.* New York: Berkley Books, 1998.

Zieghan, Suzen J. *The Stepparent's Survival Guide: A Workbook for Creating a Happy Blended Family.* Oakland, CA: New Harbinger Publications, 2002.

Zukav, Gary. *Mind of the Soul.* New York: Simon & Schuster, 2002.

Zukav, Gary. *Seat of the Soul.* New York: Simon & Schuster, 1998.

Index

ABOUT THE AUTHOR

Stephan B. Poulter is a clinical psychologist who has worked with more than 2300 fathers and sons over 23 years. He lives in Los Angeles, California.